HOUSING BY PEOPLE

HOUSING BY PEOPLE

TOWARDS AUTONOMY IN BUILDING ENVIRONMENTS

John F. C. Turner

PREFACE
by Colin Ward

PANTHEON BOOKS
NEW YORK

First American Edition

 Published in the United States by Pantheon Books, a division of Random House, Inc., New York. Originally published in Great Britain as *Housing by People: Towards Autonomy in Building Environments* by Marion Boyars Publishers Ltd., London.

Library of Congress Cataloging in Publication Data

Turner, John F.C.
Housing by People.

Includes bibliographical references.
1. Housing I. Title.
HD7287.5.T86 1977 301.5'4 76-27747
ISBN 0-394-40902-7
ISBN 0-394-73258-8 pbk.

Manufactured in the United States of America

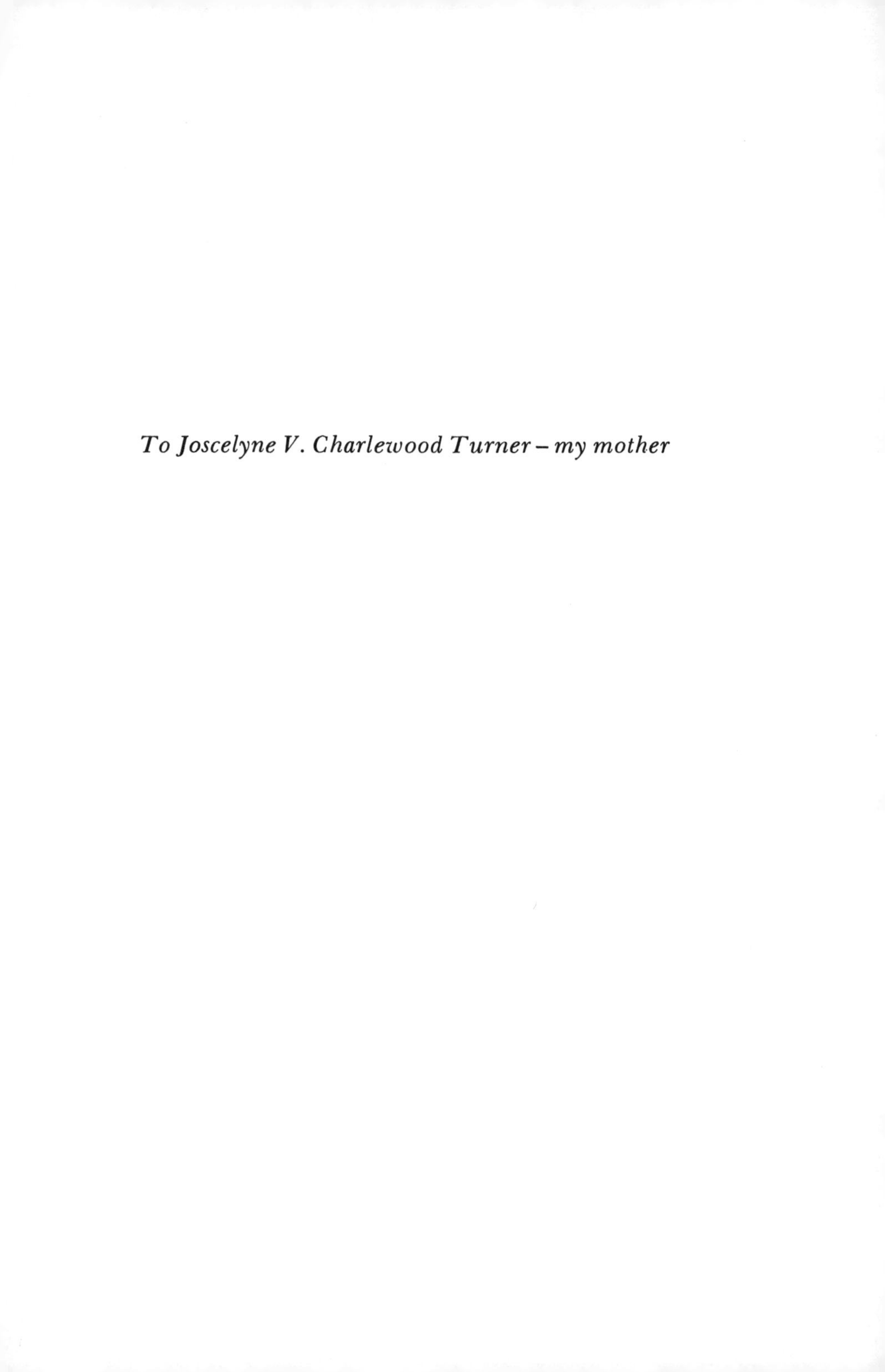

To Joscelyne V. Charlewood Turner – my mother

CONTENTS

ACKNOWLEDGEMENTS

I might never have made this start on organizing my observations and ideas without Monica Pidgeon's irresistable support. Monica swept me into writing my first essays on housing after a tour of the *barriadas* of Lima which we contemplated together while standing on the ruined Incaic citadel of Pachacamac just fourteen years ago. Thanks to her own and Pat Crooke's heroic editorship, *Dwelling Resources in Latin America* appeared as a special issue of *Architectural Design* in August, 1963. Although some of the papers I wrote since may now be better known, that number of *Architectural Design* committed me to the work that Monica has encouraged ever since. Its continuation now appears in this working paper, thanks to the obligation to write a chapter during each of the past eight months so that the first draft could be serialized in *Architectural Design* – the first being the last issues under Monica's editorship and the rest being the first under her successors, Martin Spring and Haig Beck. I am especially grateful to Haig whose enthusiasm is as infectious as Monica's; without his extremely hard work it would have been impossible to complete this book in time for the Vancouver Conference on Human Settlements to which this is offered as a contribution to the discussion of the basic issues. It is also probable that this work would never have continued without Ivan Illich's generous encouragement and timely chidings and his recommendation to Marion Boyars that I should be contracted to write a book in this 'Ideas In Progress' series. To her, who edited, and Caryl McAlonan, who produced this book, my sincere thanks. This coincidence of extraordinarily supportive friends and publishers has made it possible for me to overcome my resistance to embarking on a synthesis of ideas that have grown out of my working life and friendships in Peru, and which my friends in the United States helped me develop afterwards.

When I first met Monica Pidgeon, I had already been working for six years in Peru, sometimes in highland villages but mainly in the self-built and self-governing urban *barriadas* where so many of the most active villagers finally settle. My deepest debt, of course, is to them and to my Peruvian co-workers who gave me the opportunity of learning from the Peruvian people. I cannot possibly mention even a fraction of those whom I knew and with whom I was privileged to live and work. Special thanks are due to Eduardo Neira Alva, who suggested the idea of going to Peru and to Luis Ortiz de Zevallos who provided the opportunity to teach in his pioneering institute of planning in Lima. I am also especially indebted to Hernan Bedoya Forga of Arequipa, with whom I spent much of the first and happiest years – we even founded a new and now flourishing *pueblo joven* together, the day after the earthquake of January 15, 1958. While these friends must represent my many professional colleagues, Senor and Senora Romero of Tres Compuertas, Lima, must represent the very many friends (and teachers) I found among the citizens we were endeavouring to serve. The self-sacrificing Romeros neglected the building of their own house while I knew them, although they gave more time than they could afford to help others to get theirs, not only in Lima but in small towns such as Pativilca, where I first met them in 1960.

As a direct result of the August 1963 special number of *Architectural Design* I met the late Charles Abrams through Donald Appleyard, at MIT. And shortly afterwards Lloyd Rodwin offered me a research associateship at the Joint Center for Urban Studies of MIT and Harvard University. This gave me the opportunity to carry out a field study in Lima – with Marcia Koth de Paredes' invaluable assistance

– and to write several widely circulated papers in 1966 and 1967, the most important and influential of which was prepared with Rolf Goetze's help. (*Uncontrolled Urban Settlements Problems and Policies*; originally prepared as a working paper for the United Nations Seminar on Urbanization, Pittsburgh, October 1966). It was only through the intensive and wide as well as deep study of self-help and owner-built housing in the USA under Donald Schon that my North American friends and I began to see the common denominators of our First and Third World experiences. These observations are presented in *Freedom to Build,* the only form in which the work of the group is readily available. This preliminary version of *Housing by People* is an attempt to develop the cross-cultural comparisons and general principles of that jointly authored work. For their own contributions and assistance in the clarification of my own ideas, I must thank the co-editor of *Freedom to Build*, Robert Fichter, and co-authors Rolf Goetze, Peter Grenell, William Grindley, Hans Harms, Richard Spohn and Ian Donald Terner.

The immediate precursor of the present book is the work initiated together with Tomasz Sudra in Mexico. A very substantial part of the data base for *Housing by People* is contained in Tomasz' dissertation (for a Ph.D. at the Department of Urban Studies and Planning at MIT). Indeed, he should be considered as a co-author of the central chapters (on the issues of value, economy, and authority) which rely heavily on information obtained by Tomasz and his Mexican students. We are currently working together on further studies and jointly anticipate entering into a correspondence with readers on the development of these shared ideas.

John F Charlewood Turner

London
February 1976

INTRODUCTION TO THE AMERICAN EDITION

As my American friends and I discovered, or rediscovered, there is still a great deal of housing by people in the United States. While it is true that North Americans have less freedom to build than their counterparts in Peru and Mexico, they have more than most Europeans, including the British. In fact, despite very different contexts, we found that the ways and means, the costs and benefits involved in building in North and South America are remarkably similar.

In this preface to the US edition of *Housing by People,* I plan to outline the American precedents which flowed into my own experiences in Peru to create the foundations for this book. In addition, this introduction is meant to correct the false impression which many readers will already have from the book's title. Both this book and its precursor, *Freedom to Build,*[1] are, of course, about self-help, but in a wider and deeper sense than that commonly used by the contemporary 'self-help housing' lobby, and in a very different sense from that of Samuel Smiles. Autonomy in building environments means self-help – that is, self-determination at the local level where a person still retains his or her identity.[2] However, self-help, if limited to a narrow

[1] Edited by the author with Robert Fichter, and co-authored with six other colleagues, *Freedom to Build* was published by Macmillan, New York, in 1972.

[2] I refer mainly to the work of Abraham H. Maslow. See *The Farther Reaches of Human Nature,* published posthumously in 1971 by Viking Press, New York.

do-it-yourself sense, or even to group construction, can actually reduce autonomy by making excessive demands on personal time and energy and by reducing household mobility. In other words, I am no more advocating individual self-sufficiency, or autarchy, than the sort of autarchic or authoritarian rule of centrally administered organizations – to which Samuel Smiles's capitalistic version of self-help so rapidly leads.

By clarifying the relationships between North and South American building experiences, and their relevance to British and other European situations, I hope to avoid both left and right misinterpretations of my views on public housing. To condemn heteronomy in housing, to point out the material diseconomies, social dysfunctions, and general counter-productivity of centrally administered housing supply systems, does not mean that I feel government has no role. A careful reading of this book will show that what I am advocating is a radical change of relations between people and government in which government ceases to persist in doing what it does badly or uneconomically – building and managing houses – and concentrates on what it has the authority to do: to ensure equitable access to resources which local communities and people cannot provide for themselves. To fight instead for the restoration or extension of public expenditure on conventional housing programmes is as reactionary as the failure to press for land reform and the liberation of housing finance from corporate banking.

Believers in heteronomy, from the corporate-capitalist right to the state-capitalist left, are bound to regard owner-builders in an urban-industrial setting as anomalous vestiges of the past. They will also see the squatter-settlers of the Third World either as an aberration and a cancer or as a symptom of injustice, to be removed by force in either case with bulldozers and police or by chopping off and changing the heads of state. On the other hand, those who have little or no confidence in the housing capability of centrally administered systems will see the signs of an alternate future in the surviving US owner-builders[3] and in the burgeoning squatter-settlers of the Third World.[4] Neither conservative nor radical authoritarians see any significant connections between these owner-builders and squatter-settlers. Both assume that the poor squatter-settler must be led into urban-industrial consumer society, though each differs somewhat on the method to be used. However, those of us who reject that consumer society's values and whose sense of insecurity increases as we observe our growing dependency on pyramidal structures, centralizing technologies and non-renewable resources, look to the immense achievements of the poor for ways out of the megatechnic trap.[5]

Interestingly enough, the relatively rich US owner-builders (along with the self-help rehabilitators and co-operative tenant-managers described below) teach the same basic lessons as the far poorer squatter-settlers of Peru and most other so-called developing countries. Because housing decisions are controlled by households themselves, or by local associations and enterprises, they generate a great deal of wealth in proportion to their income.[6] Not only do those

[3] See William Grindley, *Survivors with a Future,* Ch. 1 of *Freedom to Build,* op. cit.

[4] Of the many articles and books on contemporary urban settlement in the Third World, the most informative from my own point of view are William P. Mangin, *Peasants in Cities: Readings in the Anthropology of Urbanization,* Houghton Mifflin, Boston, 1970; and D. J. Dwer, *Housing in Third World Cities,* Longmans, London, 1975.

[5] This is an adaptation of Lewis Mumford's apposite term.

[6] The significance of ratios between income and monetary value is discussed in Chapter 3, where it is shown how so many with low and very low incomes can achieve twice the relative level of material wealth set by the commonly applied standards of mortgage banks for middle- and high-income borrowers in wealthy societies.

housed through locally self-governing systems have higher-standard homes than those provided by unsubsidized, centrally administered systems, but they have far healthier social environments than their heteronomous substitutes, whether subsidized or not. The evidence of cases like Pruitt-Igoe (Fig. 12) and Co-op City shows how much material waste and human alienation can be produced by centrally administered systems. Instead of generating wealth, heteronomy often produces poverty even among those it supplies. In any case, by suppressing local organizations, local enterprises, and personal and community initiative, it proves itself counter-productive. Comparing the cities that the poor build[7] with the 'redevelopment' schemes built to 'rehabilitate' the poor, one could paraphrase Churchill: Never in urban history did so many of the poor do so much with so little; and never before did so few of the rich do so little with so much.

The central proposition of *Freedom to Build* was that, for a viable housing process to exist, local and personal control is essential. This proposition was formulated after the discovery that the material savings and human benefits of owner building, rehabilitation, and improvement in the United States could be traced to dense local communication and supply networks open to local residents. As long as building plots or vacant buildings were available at reasonable prices and not inflated by speculation or monopolistic aggregation; as long as there was a plentiful supply of appropriate tools and materials through local distributors who did not discriminate against small or non-professional purchasers; and as long as local banks gave credit and were not absorbed into impersonally administered national corporations: then individual households and small groups could maximize the use of their own resources.

[7] See the chapter by Bryan Roberts and the author in Rosemary Righter and Peter Wilsher, *The Exploding Cities,* Proceedings of the Sunday Times and United Nations Conference in Oxford, 1974, Andre Deutsch, London, 1975.

I first grasped this key, the necessity for networks, while thinking through the reasons for owner-builders' successes with Donald Schon and our research team during our evaluation of self-help housing in the United States.[8] On further reflection I realized that the same principle underlay the squatter-settlers' successes – from the initial clandestine organizational steps among inner-city neighbours to the subsequent acquisition of cheap building materials and the hiring of skilled artisans recommended by neighbours in their new settlements. The successes of the Better Rochester Living (New York) self-help rehabilitation program, reported by Rolf Goetze in the same evaluation study,[9] were due in part to the access which the organizers had to knowledge of suitable properties on the market, and which they and the self-helpers had to skilled labour and materials suppliers. The successes of the tenant take-overs of landlord-abandoned apartment buildings in New York City, and those of the urban homesteaders in that and other US cities,[10] also depend on the advice of experienced peers and knowledge of material resources which they get mainly through networks of personal contacts.

Learning from experience and making-do with what is at hand obviously depend on personal conversation and correspondence. No one person has to know many others very well, as long as there are plenty of connections between various sets of friends. Naturally, then, the channelling of communications through hierarchically organized centres reduces personal contact, knowledge of available resources,

[8] See footnote 6 to Chapter 8, p. 148 below.

[9] See Ch. 3 of *Freedom to Build,* op. cit.

[10] See Robert Kolodny, *Self-Help in the Inner City: A Study of Lower-Income Cooperative Housing Conversion in New York,* privately published by United Neighborhood Houses of New York, Inc., 101 East 15th Street, New York, N.Y. 10003. Further and more recent information can be obtained from Philip St. Georges, Director, The Urban Homesteading Assistance Board, Cathedral House, 1047 Amsterdam Avenue, New York, N.Y. 10025.

and therefore, opportunities to experience, learn, and increase the availability of resources for others.

The owner-builders and the squatter-settlers, along with the practitioners of many other forms of locally controlled building and improvement, achieve their savings and match their infinitely variable demands with the access they have to locally available resources. They can use their own initiative and skills of negotiation (if they are just buying) and of organization (if they are directing construction) and their manual skills and labor (if they are also building), as long as the essential resources are locally available. In all successful cases observed, suitable building sites or existing buildings were available in appropriate locations and at reasonable prices. Suitable building materials and tools were at hand, along with people able and willing to provide the skills and time required. Credit, where needed, was also available under acceptable conditions.

The supply systems for these essential resources – and the financial means for obtaining them – are necessarily locally based and independent of outside control. Although overlapping and complementary, the networks of contacts giving access to each system are distinct. Every user, whether an individual or a small organization, makes its own entry and carries out its own, often unique program. Only in this way can all available resources be used or mobilized – whether they are small, scattered, and irregular plots of land; odd lots of otherwise wasted materials; un- or underemployed people; or simply the imagination and initiative to combine any of these.

As soon as the communications network, or network of networks, breaks down, or is rendered impotent by the monopolization of resources by centralized organizations or institutions, the range and amount of accessible resources shrink. As the owner-builder research team found in a New Hampshire town, this can happen just through the centralization of banking. The absorption of a local bank by a national corporation and the appointment of an outsider as manager eliminated the major local source of mortgage finance in that town. Unlike the previous manager, who knew every borrower, or at least his relatives or employers, and who accepted owner-building as an established and reliable tradition, the new big-business-minded manager from out of town knew no one and had the usual prejudices about practices that limit the scope of expanding businesses.

The larger an organization, the less concern it will have for individual and small-community demands. For such an organization, it always seems more profitable, or anyway less troublesome, to deal with a few large developers. The invasion of New Hampshire by vacation- and second-home buyers is, of course, welcomed by the big-business interests it stimulates. Neither need care about the natives who can no longer afford to keep their family lands or homes and who are often forced to live on tiny rented sites in tinny mobile homes that rapidly lose value.[11]

In the United States, the experiences of inner-city rehabilitation and tenant management show that the same principles apply in high-density urban areas as in small towns and suburbs. The cases described below show that the critical issue is not the choice between private business and public welfare but between network and hierarchic organizations. Better Rochester Living (BRL) was evaluated against a non-profit program, set up at the same time in the same area, for the same types of houses, on the same scale.[12]

[11] The Center for Auto Safety, *Mobile Homes: The Low-Cost Housing Hoax,* Grossman, New York, 1975. Readers should know that my colleague Ian Donald Terner, who has written extensively on industrialized building, is critical of this book for its failure to point out the positive benefits mobile homes can provide. In the first place, they are very easy for lower-income people to buy. For many, especially the elderly, durability may be relatively unimportant; and, as many will have observed in rural areas, mobile homes often form the core of a conventional house, in which case they are fully protected and can last indefinitely.

[12] Rolf Goetze in *Freedom to Build,* op. cit.

A

Figs. A, B. Sweat equity: urban homesteading on the Lower East Side, New York, N.Y. (Photos by East 11th Street Housing Movement.)

B

The CPT Housing Corporation was organized by a non-profit agency as a conventional rental project. It employed a general contractor to work in the conventional way. BRL, on the other hand, involved the future owner-occupiers both in the selection of their own homes and in the rehabilitation work itself. They were encouraged to do all that they were capable of doing themselves. Measured against CPT's costs, the savings from the self-management and self-build inputs of each household, from the elimination of a general contractor's overheads and profit (which have to be generous enough to balance the risks of rehabilitation work), and from the reduction of professional costs and managerial overheads, when added to BRL's skill in finding and buying properties, prove a striking yardstick for its success. BRL's costs for 14 units averaged $10,974; CTP's costs averaged $18,600 for 9 units.

Similarly dramatic cost differences have been achieved in the Urban Homestead Assistance Board (U-HAB) program in New York City, for much the same reasons. U-HAB was set up following the publication of *Freedom to Build* and directed by Ian Donald Terner, a co-author. Its purpose is to support and extend the spontaneous tenant take-overs of apartment buildings abandoned by landlords unable to profit from or even maintain their properties as a result of rising property taxes, increasing restrictions on and consequent costs of improvements, and falling incomes from frozen rents. Concerned and observant citizens in touch with grass-roots organizing efforts found many spontaneous cases of tenant take-overs uselessly repeating the mistakes of other organizers in the same city, and very often in the same neighbourhood. U-HAB was set up to overcome this wasteful isolation and to support initiatives within the New York City administration to provide financial and technical assistance for these incipient co-operatives. At the time of writing, after two years of operation, U-HAB has assisted groups taking over more than 60 buildings, 50 of which are fully organized and providing improved housing for more than 2,000 people in over 600 apartments. Initial costs, to quote the 1975 annual report, range between $8,000 and $13,000 per unit, with monthly carrying charges of $80 to $180. This is less than half the cost of comparable commercial rehabilitation, and about one-quarter the cost and rental price of new units.

Projects like BRL and U-HAB, where great material savings have been made, are carried out by three sets of actors: the participants and eventual users themselves, the funding agency (usually governmental), and independent specialists (usually from a non-profit agency). While this combination may be essential at present, the deeper reason for the measurable savings, as well as the equally evident but non-quantifiable human benefits, lies in the meaning of the activity itself. The main motive for personally committing oneself to the always exacting and often exhausting job of organizing and managing, let alone self-building, may be the bodily need for socially acceptable shelter, but 'higher' needs for creative expression and personal identity are, in most cases, also present and for many equally important.[13] No self-helper to whom I have ever spoken, and no observer whose evaluations I have read, has failed to emphasize the pride of achievement, the self-confidence and self-respect, or the delight in creativity, however hard the task may have been. I am sure that it is this existential wholeness – the simultaneous satisfaction of the universal need for physical shelter, the cultural need for belonging to a particular society and the highly differentiated and personal need for self-expression – that gives housing its special meaning when

[13] William Grindley, in a subsequent study of 121 owner-builders in Boston's suburbs ("The Suburban Owner Builder," a case study of owner-building in Boston's suburbs, Master of City Planning thesis, MIT, 1972), found that only 30 per cent failed to emphasize non-economic motives for undertaking the work. These other motives had to do with style, quality, desire to build, and simply having the ability.

done at the level of personal and community action.[14] Although there may be no analytical way to prove it, it is obvious to me that both economy and conviviality can come about only through personal responsibility.

This necessary emphasis on the relationships between inner and outer, use- and market-values, tends to focus the meaning of autonomy in housing on relatively extreme forms of self-help. This should be corrected by zeroing in on the more limited, but cumulatively more important, issue of management and maintenance. In highly urbanized countries with slow-growing or stable populations, fewer and fewer households build or move into new homes. To an increasing extent, housing economy depends on careful management and maintenance of the existing stock; and this, in turn, depends on personal care and responsibility as much as, or even more than, on new construction.

The partial dynamiting of the relatively new, modern, architectural-award-winning Pruitt-Igoe project in St. Louis, Missouri (Fig. 12) was the watershed for centrally administered housing-supply systems. Confidence in these building and management forms started to collapse with this first and traumatic demolition. Its image constantly reappears in publications and films on modern housing, now almost always critical. The drama of its significance is heightened when contrasted with the tenant management of neighbouring projects.

Without any changes in the structures themselves, the formerly deteriorating Darst and Carr Square housing projects, which were rapidly approaching the irreparable condition of neighbouring Pruitt-Igoe, are now being revived and regenerated by the tenants themselves. When a third rent increase was announced by the St. Louis Housing

[14] This distinction between three 'levels' of needs was relayed to me at the Centre for Alternatives in Urban Development Summer School in August, 1976, by Philippe Theunissen, from the work of Henri Labourit in *L'Homme et la Ville*, Flammarion, Paris, 1971.

Authority for early 1969, after two increases the previous year, the tenants started a nine-month rent strike. The tenants were already infuriated by the escalating rents and deteriorating conditions. Some families were spending as much as 60 per cent of their incomes on rent alone for badly maintained, increasingly vandalized, and crime-ridden housing. Self-organized through the strike action, the tenants won their demands to limit rents to 25 per cent of household income and to share control of the Authority's administration. By 1975, the Authority had handed the administration of four of the city's seven projects over to Tenant Management Corporations, with 2,600 units in their charge. The St. Louis Housing Authority now acts as a holding company which contracts with the TMCs for the day-to-day administration the Authority used to carry out itself. As in the New York tenant take-overs – which went much further by leading to co-operative ownership – assistance was provided by an independent third party (in this case, the Ford Foundation).

During the first two years of tenant management, 'Carr Square maintained average monthly rent collections, including back rents, of 100.1 per cent. Darst's average was 99.1 per cent.'[15] The TMCs have their own maintenance and (male and female) security staffs employing previously unemployed tenants. Elevators now work, grounds are well kept, crime and vandalism have dropped sharply, and many formerly uninhabitable apartments have been repaired and are now occupied. By March 1973, Carr Square occupancies had increased by 6 per cent to 99.2 per cent; Darst, by 8 per cent to 67.1 per cent.

As Colin Ward reports in his book *Tenants Take Over,*

[15] From the film *The Walls Come Tumbling Down,* by Madeline Anderson/Onyx Productions, distributed in the USA by Phoenix Films Inc., 470 Park Avenue South, New York, N.Y. 10016. The film and a pamphlet were produced for the Ford Foundation.

even in the United States[16] St. Louis was not the first city to accept and facilitate tenant management. The TMC of Boston was set up in 1966. But the pioneering and often cited case is from Oslo, where the tenants of a once deteriorating and despised project have become the co-operative owners of now desirable blocks of flats. As this is written, the dramatic tenants' struggle in the so-called Co-op City continues.[17] This monstrous development in the Bronx, New York City, has 35 high-rise buildings with a population of 60,000. It was built under a State program (the Mitchell-Lama plan) for the provision of low-income housing in areas of special need. The initially enthusiastic residents had to pass a means test. But, as in the St. Louis case, rapidly escalating rents precipitated a strike. The mortgage proved to be nearly double what the tenants had been led to believe, and payments had risen 60 per cent during the first five years. In April 1975, the tenants were hit with another increase, this time of 33⅓ per cent, as a first instalment on an 82 per cent increase over the coming five years. The following month the tenants collected their own rents and deposited 80 per cent of the total due on the State Governor's desk in protest. A year later 80 per cent of the tenants were still depositing their rents in an escrow account and were challenging the banks to foreclose – facing them with the equally impractical alternatives of evicting tens of thousands of people by force or going through the courts case by case.

The organizational capability demonstrated by the tenants has proved formidable. General policy and planning are determined by a steering committee composed of representatives of the buildings and the civic associations, and

[16] Colin Ward, *Tenants Take Over,* Architectural Press, London, 1975.

[17] See Vivian Gornick, *The 60,000 Rent Strikers At Co-op City,* in Liberation, Spring 1976 (special double issue on the New York City Crisis), 339 Lafayette Street, New York, N.Y. 10012.

of ethnic and age groups. (The residents are 75 per cent white—largely Jewish—and 25 per cent black and Puerto Rican.) The development is organized by areas, each building having its own management. In the spring of 1976, a communications center was printing and distributing 16,000 bulletins daily, and providing a 24-hour hot-line telephone service. During the first ten days of every month, 1,500 volunteers collected rents from 7 to 9 P.M. in 75 building lobbies. Whatever the final outcome, the managerial capacity of the tenants has shown how unnecessary the previous paternalistic and remote management was in the first place. Of course, these events do not prove that such huge schemes are non-viable under any form of management, but they do suggest how very large developments could be broken down into manageable sections and co-operatively administered. This would minimize resentment, carelessness, and managerial costs by maximizing responsibility and awareness. Again, this is not a solution to the basic financial problem created by the public authorities when they insist on building such expensive and inflationary structures. When contrasted with the co-operative tenant take-over of the plentiful supply of abandoned buildings of humane scale – over 100,000 dwellings available in New York City by early 1975 – Co-op City is clearly as insane as it looks.

The basic lessons to be drawn from contemporary housing experience in the United States are no different from those in the rest of the world. Even if big housing developments do not look hideous to everyone, they are hideously expensive and socially destructive. Whether in the United States or elsewhere, both material and human viability evidently demand a small scale, social and physical diversity, and variety. It is equally clear that this can only be provided, and sustained, by large numbers of responsibly self-governing persons, co-operating groups, and small local enterprises. The re-awakening of such common-sense knowledge, which can be applied to many areas in addition to housing, may not be as easy in North as in South America, or in other regions where capital-intensive technologies and highly paid managements clearly cannot meet more than a small proportion of the demand – and even more clearly are regressive when they try. After Pruitt-Igoe and Co-op City, and with the deteriorating condition of centrally administered housing in Europe increasingly visible, there are reasons to expect the early development of radically different policies in the United States.

Rolf Goetze, co-author of *Freedom to Build,* introduces his recent book, based on his work with the Boston Redevelopment Authority, with the following statement:[18]

> In the wake of ambitious urban programs and turmoil of the 1960s, a new style of planning is emerging that is tempered by the harsher economic realities of today, and that demonstrates a humanistic approach that promises to radically modify the practices of the past. This new 'planning' concentrates on people, perceptions, and ethnic considerations, and is based on understanding the dynamics of residential migration and the forces unleashed in neighbourhood pluralism. This new approach is effectively coming to supplant the earlier planning focus on hard numbers–housing stock, condition, needs for fix-up and replacement. In the last decade planners increasingly vied for federal assistance, outdoing each other in calling attention to their urban problems until nearly everyone accepted the rhetoric that without federal dollars the end of our urban areas is in sight.

Only those who make such assumptions will suppose that this book represents a reaction against government intervention, rather than a demand for a change in its nature. I join with all those who, like Rolf Goetze, insist that govern-

[18] Rolf Goetze, *Building Neighbourhood Confidence: A Humanistic Strategy for Urban Housing,* Ballinger, Cambridge, Mass., 1976.

ment must stop sapping people's confidence in themselves and in their neighbourhoods; that it must instead support personal and local enterprise and development. This, of course, means a new alliance of people and government against heteronomous corporations, whether national or multi-national.

PREFACE

The moment that housing, a universal human activity, becomes defined as a problem, a housing problems industry is born, with an army of experts, bureaucrats and researchers, whose existence is a guarantee that the problem won't go away. John F. C. Turner is something much rarer than a housing expert: he is a philosopher of housing, seeking answers to questions which are so fundamental that they seldom get asked.

He is one of a group of thinkers who, working in different fields, often unknown to each other, have brought from the poor countries of the world lessons of immense value for the rich countries, lessons which are universal. For many years after the second world war it was assumed that the rich countries had an immense contribution of technical and organizational wisdom to bestow on the 'under-developed' or 'developing' nations: a one-way trip of know-how and high technology. Aid became a cold-war weapon and a vehicle of economic and ideological imperialism. Then, slowly, voices emerged which stated the issues in an entirely different way.

When E.F. Schumacher and his colleagues started the Intermediate Technology Development Group, to locate or design machines and tools that would help countries with a superfluity of labour and a shortage of capital, they were concerned with the real needs of the poor countries, but they gradually realized the importance of the principles they evolved for the poor areas of the rich world, and finally they came to see that they had formulated principles of universal application: intermediate technology became alternative technology. Paulo Freire and Ivan Illich, attempting to come to grips with the educational needs of Latin American countries, stumbled on truths which have changed the nature of the continuing debate on education throughout the world.

John Turner absorbed in Peru the lessons offered by illegal squatter settlements: that far from being the threatening symptoms of social malaise, they were a triumph of self-help which, overcoming the culture of poverty, evolved over time into fully serviced suburbs, giving their occupants a foothold in the urban economy. More perhaps than anyone else, he has changed the way we perceive such settlements. It was his paper at the 1966 United Nations seminar on Uncontrolled Urban Settlements[1] that was most influential in setting in motion governmental 'site-and-services' housing programmes – policies about which he himself has reservations. He evolved an ideology of housing applicable to the exploding cities of the Third World. But when he moved from South to North America, having been invited to the Joint Center for Urban Studies of the Massachusetts Institute of Technology and Harvard University, he found that the ideas he had formulated in Peru were also true of the richest nation in the world, and when he returned to England after seventeen years abroad, he found that the housing situation in Britain too fitted his formulation. He was, perhaps to his surprise, expressing universal truths about housing.

Turner is not a great believer in the value of books, (the present work was wrung out of him by Ivan Illich's admonition that he was burying his ideas under a lot of Peruvian mud bricks), but out of his past writings and speeches I have, without any authorization from him, distilled Turner's three laws of housing. Turner's Second Law says that the important thing about housing is not what it *is*, but what it *does* in people's lives, in other words that dweller satisfaction is not necessarily related to the

[1] *Uncontrolled Urban Settlements: Problems and Policies,* a working paper for the United Nations Seminar on Urbanization Problems and Policies, University of Pennsylvania, Pittsburgh, October 1966

imposition of standards. Turner's Third Law says that deficiencies and imperfections in *your* housing are infinitely more tolerable if they are your responsibility than if they are *somebody else's*. But beyond the psychological truths of the second and third laws, are the social and economic truths of Turner's First Law, which I take from the book *Freedom to Build*[2]:

> 'When dwellers control the major decisions and are free to make their own contribution to the design, construction or management of their housing, both the process and the environment produced stimulate individual and social well-being. When people have no control over, nor responsibility for key decisions in the housing process, on the other hand, dwelling environments may instead become a barrier to personal fulfillment and a burden on the economy.'

This is a carefully-worded statement that says no more and no less than it means. Notice that he says 'design, construction *or* management'. He is not implying, as critics sometimes suggest, that the poor of the world should become do-it-yourself housebuilders, though of course in practice they very often have to be. He *is* implying that they should be in control. It is sometimes said of his approach to housing that it represents a kind of Victorian idealization of self-help, relieving governments of their responsibilities so far as housing is concerned, and that it is therefore what Marxists would no doubt describe as objectively reactionary. But that is not his position. He lives in the real world, and however much he, like me, would enjoy living in an anarchist society, he knows that in our world resources are in the control of governmental or propertied elites. Consequently he concludes that 'while local control over necessarily diverse personal and local goods and services – such as housing – is essential, local control depends on

[2]John F. C. Turner and Robert Fichter eds., *Freedom to Build*, Collier Macmillan, New York, 1972

personal and local access to resources which only central government can guarantee'.

And even when governments make no such guarantees, it is clear that the poor in some (though by no means all) of the exploding cities of the Third World, often have a freedom of manouevre which has been totally lost by the poor of the decaying cities of the rich world, who are deprived of the last shred of personal autonomy and human dignity, because they have nothing they can depend on apart from the machinery of welfare. In London, Glasgow, New York or Detroit, in spite of an enormous investment in mass housing, the poor are trapped in the culture of poverty. But in the unofficial, informal sector of the economy of 'the cities the poor build'[3] in Africa or Latin America, what Turner calls the 'lateral information and decision networks' enable them to draw on resources that the rich nations have forgotten about. Governments put their faith not in popular involvement, but in the vertical and hierarchical organization of large-scale works and services, but 'when these centralized systems are used to house the poor, their scale and the limitations of management rule out the essential variety and flexibility of housing options; even if the planners were sensitive to and could have access to the fine-grain information on which local housing decisions are made, it would be administratively impossible to use it'.

One irony is that when John Turner or his colleague Patrick Crooke, are commissioned by international agencies to report on housing strategies for particular 'developing countries' they urge governments to increase people's access to resources rather than grandiose housing projects, but find that while the agencies generally accept this advice, many governments reject it. They cannot believe that what poor people do for themselves can be right

[3]Rosemary Righter and Peter Wilsher, *The Exploding Cities*, Andre Deutsch, London, 1975

and proper.

People with a political or professional vested interest in the housing problems industry find it difficult to place Turner's message on the ideological spectrum. As he says, 'the common debate is between the conventional left which condemns capitalism and the conventional right which condemns personal dependency upon state institutions. I agree with both, so nobody committed to either side can agree with me'. But his return to Britain in 1973 was well-timed. For in Britain this was the year that saw the lowest level of house-building for decades, (just as in the United States it was the year that saw the withdrawal of Federal aid for housing). Housing policy in Britain rests on a very crude duopoly: owner-occupation financed by mortgage loans (53%) and publicly rented housing (33%) with a dwindling private landlord sector, usually of sub-standard housing. This paucity of choice leaves a large section of the population with no way of getting housed – hence the rise and the legitimacy of the squatter's movement. In the public sector there is a crisis of finance, of maintenance and of management. Provided at great expense it fails to give commensurate satisfaction for its occupants who have been rigidly excluded from decision-making and control.

In the years since 1973 there has been a rapid change in the way in which housing issues are perceived in Britain, a change which has even penetrated governmental thinking. A demand has arisen, not just for the consultation of tenants, but for tenant control, for the transfer of both publicly and privately rented housing to tenants' co-operatives, for dweller-controlled rehabilitation, for self-build housing associations, for widening the range of options open to people. Turner has been in the midst of a network of activists in all these fields, just as he is the pre-eminent British link with a world-wide network of advocates of alternatives in housing. Out of his own and his friends' experience he has evolved the alternative philosophy that is set out in this book.

Some readers will perceive that the approach to housing outlined here, from a very rich fund of examples and case-histories, fits into a general framework of ideas. They are right. I have known the author intermittently for a quarter of a century, and I can see that it was inevitable that he should emerge as the most authoritative and persuasive advocate of housing by people. In the 1970s his analysis fits like a finger in a glove the climate of opinion moulded by such writers as Paul Goodman, Ivan Illich and Fritz Schumacher. We hardly need to ask what the author's opinions are on industry, work, leisure, agriculture or education. But the shaping of a mind which is actually receptive to the experience of poor families in far-away countries, their own struggles and aspirations, has deeper roots. I think that there is a background to Tuner's receptivity. As a schoolboy he was given the task of summarizing a chapter from Lewis Mumford's *The Culture of Cities*[4]. This encounter led him to the work of Mumford's mentor, Patrick Geddes, whose book *Cities in Evolution*, written in the years leading up to the first world war, is really a handbook on the involvement of the citizen in environmental decision-making. Decades ago John Turner contributed to an appendix to the 1949 reprint of Geddes' book[5]. He was then a student at the Architectural Association School of Architecture in London, having been seduced from military service by the anarchist newspaper *Freedom*, whose founder, Peter Kropotkin is another of the formative ideological influences in Turner's life. In 1948 I translated for *Freedom* an article from the Italian anarchist journal *Volonta* by the architect Giancarlo de Carlo, which attempted to formulate an anarchist approach to housing. I

[4] Lewis Mumford, *The Culture of Cities*, Secker & Warburg, London, 1938

[5] Patrick Geddes, ed. by Jacqueline Tyrwhitt (2nd edition), *Cities In Evolution*, Williams & Norgate, London 1949

am happy that he was one of our readers, and when Turner, de Carlo, Pat Crooke and I first met in Venice in 1952, we discussed the crucial issue of 'who provides and who decides?' in housing and planning. In our different ways and in totally different circumstances, we have all been faithful to this anarchist approach to the fundamental issue of housing, and just in case anyone should suggest that John Turner's book is simply a reaction to the total bankruptcy of housing policy in all countries, rich or poor, I am glad to testify that it is the result of a lifetime of involvement in issues which are central to the hopes and happiness of ordinary people everywhere.

London
February 1976

Colin Ward

HOUSING BY PEOPLE

1. WHO DECIDES?

The Central Issue

The sometimes true story about the architects and planners who preserve some of the slums that are cleared to make way for their schemes, in order to have somewhere pleasant to live themselves, has a moral which is the theme of this working paper. The recent publication of an issue of the *Journal of the Royal Institute of British Architects* with the word CRISIS in red letters the height of its black cover, and the decision of homeless working-class families to take over a vacant block of Council flats in the East End of London, are typical indicators of the simultaneous loss of confidence in the ways we have been building by those who decide and those who have to live with it. The moral is simple and old enough to be forgotten by most of us most of the time. As the traditional words put it: Do unto others as you would have them do unto you. It is a shock to think that this might apply to all of us all of the time, even when we are acting as officially certified experts on other people's problems. But now that architects and planners as well as the other professions are confronted with a rapidly rising consciousness of their incompetence to decide for others what is best for them, as well as the generally unpopular nature of what they design, the now rather stale joke rarely fails to provoke a nervous laugh.

Who decides what for whom is the central issue of this and other chapters to follow on housing and human settlement. It is an issue that is shared with a large and rapidly growing proportion of all who supply and receive centrally administered social services. The occasionally literal collapse and the increasingly frequent demolition of recently built public housing in highly institutionalized countries such as the United Kingdom and the United States, is paralleled by equally accelerating crises in the school systems and the health services. It is wrong to suppose that the revolt is by the dissatisfied users alone, as the RIBA report shows; those who earn their living as experts are among the most articulate critics.

No one denies the universal need for homes any more than the importance of learning or keeping in good health. But many have come to identify these ends with the ways and means that turn them into products. Housing has commonly come to mean the current stock of dwelling units and the capability of large building and management organizations to provide more. Learning is now commonly understood to be synonymous with education and this, in turn, with schooling and even with the institutions that award certificates. In the same way, good health has become bound to health services, and these in turn to hospitals. And so it goes for all everyday needs and for what must also be everyday activities if they are to be properly satisfied. The alienation of everyday life by organizations that reify activities and institutionalize their values deprives the vast majority of us, as Edward Sapir wrote: 'of any but an insignificant and culturally abortive share in the satisfaction of the immediate wants of mankind, so that we are further deprived of both opportunity and stimulation to share in the production of new utilitarian values. Part of the time we are drayhorses; the rest of the time we are listless consumers of goods which have received no least impress of our personality.'[1]

The issue of who decides and who does what for whom, is a question of *how* we house ourselves, *how* we learn, *how* we keep healthy. This discussion can only take place between

[1] Edward Sapir, *Culture, Genuine and Spurious* in Edward Sapir, *Culture, Language and Personality, Selected Essays,* ed. by David G. Mandelbaum, University of California Press, Berkeley, California, 1954

those who can separate the ways and means from the ends, and who are therefore able to question the commercialized or institutionalized values of modern societies.

The chapters that follow are about two sets of ways and means – the ways and means of centrally administrated systems, and those of self-governing, local systems. These ways and means generate very different immediate ends, which are the things that concern us in the first place.

Richard Barnet and Ronald Müller ask the key question: 'Can we organize the planet through centralizing technologies into ever-larger pyramidal structures?'[2] If the environments resulting from such systems are an indication of the results they produce in other spheres of life, then the answer is 'No'. Only a rich minority can be supplied in these centrally administered ways using centralizing technologies, and then only at the expense of an impoverished majority and the rapid exhaustion or poisoning of the planet's resources. This 'supreme political issue of our time', as Barnet and Müller rightly call it, is the choice between heteronomy (other-determined) and autonomy (self-determined) in personal and local matters.

While it may be ridiculous to imagine a well-populated world without world-wide organizations and authorities – without which telecommunication, for example, could hardly exist – it is absurd to think of a World Housing Authority centralizing humanity's supply of dwelling units. Where the absurd is a partial reality as in the internationalization of agriculture, the danger of disastrous commodity shortages has never been so great or imminent. In historical fact, good housing like plentiful food, is more common where it is locally produced through network structures and decentralizing technologies. *The thesis in this book is that these are the only ways and means through which*

[2] Richard J. Barnet and Ronald E. Müller, *Global Reach: The Power of the Multinational Corporations*, Simon & Schuster, New York, 1974

satisfactory goods and services can be obtained, and that they are vital for a stable planet.

The mirage of development

When told in a Third World context, the story of the slum conserving architects is even more relevant to our theme. An English friend, working on a job in the Middle East, told me how a firm of consultants carefully conserved, for their own use, a few buildings in the old town which they had been employed to 'redevelop'. The traditional, thick-walled courtyard houses and narrow streets provided maximum shade and natural air-conditioning. This was very sensible in view of the high costs and breakdown risks of building and living in mechanically conditioned glass and concrete structures in very hot climates. In this case, and in many countries that have only recently achieved political independence, there was no question of social upgrading. The original upper-class owners and residents had already moved out of their dense, shaded and inward-looking traditional neighbourhoods into exposed, western-style suburbs as fast as they could get their imported consultants to design and direct their construction. Unfortunately for the consultants themselves, their exceedingly hospitable Arab clients would not return to their previous homes, even to visit their guest employees. Communication between professional and client was therefore greatly reduced, though not quite as much, perhaps, as it is between the planners and designers of most modern housing developments, and those who have to live in, pay and care for them.

When reflecting on the horrors of our own urban-industrial world, or on the even more nightmarish consequences of managerial post-industrialism, we must remember that the mirage-like reflections seen by the great majority of the world's population do in fact provide glimpses of a vastly higher material standard of living. I was sharply reminded of this recently when talking to the mayor of a small, rural Middle-Eastern town who had taken a planning course in Europe and was familiar with his European wife's redeveloped home town. He was – and is – determined to turn his district of scattered peasant villages into a tourist-based city as close as possible to the alienating models we are trying to get rid of. When such clients have large sums of unstable foreign currency to spend, there are lots of opportunities for the unscrupulous (on both sides, of course). The government of this particular country has committed itself to the purchase of pre-fabricated building systems – the most uneconomic, socially dysfunctional, and materially unstable constructions ever devised.

This truly destructive mirage will fade only as the producers and users abandon the distant original models, and as those that thirst after it see how small the pool of that kind of wealth is in relation to the immense numbers crawling towards it.

There are, of course, other reasons why those disillusioned with their own ways, and trying to withdraw from their addictions, should put their own house in order before preaching to those looking forward to, or even experiencing their first intoxication. As the already considerable literature on world economy of the past ten years or so proves to all but the most entrenched or naive reactionaries, the growth of urban-industrialism is not a linear process in which the still poor will take off in the wake of their wealthy and benign tutors. It should now be clear to anyone that follows current world affairs, let alone those that study specific aspects of change in the world today, that there are but three alternative futures.

Firstly, if current rates of consumption and pollution continue, the biosphere is likely to become incapable of supporting higher forms of life long before mineral resources are exhausted. The more people who join the feast of modern consumption, the sooner this will happen. The protests against the Club of Rome's first *Limits to Growth*[3] report, boiled down to the quite reasonable conclusion that it is absurd to make such projections as there are multiple feed-backs in the over-all system (which Meadows et al grossly oversimplified), which will surely make corrections.

The kind of corrections most representatives of rich nations suggest provides the second alternative in which the rich level off their growth – but at a very high level and, implicitly, at the expense of the majority for whom there is no room at the feast and who must be kept at a much lower level to supply the others.

The third and only alternative that is both just and secure, is for the affluent society of wastemakers to reduce their levels of consumption to that which is safe for all to share. We have no right whatsoever to tell others to tighten their belts while our own bellies protrude so much that we cannot see the poverty we stand on.

It is a dismaying prospect – and a politically naive one – if it is assumed that we are fully dependent on pyramidal structures and centralizing technologies. If that were the case, the politically inconceivable but only route to survival would be a vast rationing scheme, administered by world agencies, for food, clothing, housing and all other essential services.

It is a stimulating and hopeful prospect, on the other hand, if the opposite position is taken on the supreme political issue. If the possibilities of self-governing network structures and decentralizing technologies are realized – that is, those which do not demand highly centralized production, distribution, or servicing systems – and if the intrinsically oppressive wastefulness of heteronomous struc-

[3] Donella H. Meadows, Denis L. Meadows, Jörgen Randers and William H. Behrens III, *The Limits to Growth*, Universe Books, New York, 1972

tures is also generally recognized, then those concerned with the future will take whatever action they can in order to become independent of destructively centralist organizations and thus they will institute an alternative and viable world order.

*Autonomy and heteronomy**

The partially unsolved problem is to identify the practical and necessary limits to heteronomy and its opposite, autonomy. In this and following chapters it is argued that housing and, by implication, all other personal and locally specific services, must be autonomous. It is also argued that this autonomy is far from absolute – for it depends on access to essential resources. In housing, for instance, local autonomy and direct or indirect dweller-control depend on the availability of appropriate tools and materials (or technology), of land and finance. In general, the accessibility of these basic resources is a function of law and its administration, and these, in turn are functions of central authority.

Thus we return to the traditional questions of human institutions and authority. But liberated from the distortions introduced by false expectation of mass-produced personal services, and with a vastly greater range of lightweight, low-powered, potentially decentralizing technologies the possibilities of effective action by local groups and associations, and of rapid general change, are vast and immediate. In relatively open societies such as those of Western Europe and North America this point is illustrated by the telephone.

Although most students and professional architects and planners dutifully visit their masters' and each other's works, few choose to live in them. Even those who can afford to do so seem to prefer places that were built by

**Heteronomy (2). Subjection to the rule of another being or power . . . subjection to external law opp. to autonomy. O.E.D.*

master craftsmen, artisans or ordinary folk, according to local rules and customs. How many admirers of Brasilia (Fig. 1), for example, stay there longer than necessary to see the principal buildings and, perhaps, one of the super-blocks? And how many designers of such places, prefer to spend their holidays in places like Mykonos, (Fig. 2)? The escalating prices of the diminishing supply of 'architecture without architects' limits its use to those with money[4]. And this, in the urban-industrial world, largely limits the buyers, and even transient visitors, to those that serve the organizations that inhibit and destroy what they seek with their earnings.

The more aware we become of the social costs of massive housing schemes, and of high-rise buildings, for those that cannot move about at will – the very young, the very old, and unassisted housewives – the greater are the efforts to counter the administrative and economic limitations imposed by sponsors and producers. The very wealthy can effectively demand costly simulations of traditional forms (Fig. 3), while relatively wealthy governments can often be persuaded by their advisers to balance social against additional material costs (Fig. 4). More recently, and in response to more perceptive analyses of the social psychology of alienation, as well as to direct pressures from local groups of angry voters, citizen participation has even been built into planning and building law, as in Britain; or as a prerequisite for Federal support, as in the United States. Like the variety and smallness the wealthy seek, participation also costs more when it has to be built into central agencies' programmes. The desirability of small scale, variety, and participation in highly institutionalized contexts, is not at issue. The great majority of policy-makers and administrators, planners, architects, and laymen, when they are informed, agree that it is only a

[4] Paul Rudofsky, *Architecture without Architects*, Museum of Modern Art, New York, 1963

problem of cost and productivity.

Few, however, yet raise the *issue* of the feasibility of human scale, variety, and participation or responsibility in housing and human settlement. In the view of those that take the modern system for granted, the matter rests on a mis-stated *problem* of streamlining and acceleration or of altering priorities so as to get more money from the budget.

Many of those who mistakenly suppose that the problem of housing in rich countries is lack of money or the slow pace of existing production machinery, would really like to see uniform housing estates segregating categories of people, maybe muted by the current fashion for community participation and the personalization of consumer goods and services. The more perceptive are undoubtedly comforted by the knowledge that these cost money and are therefore unlikely to survive in an inflationary world. The real test of who stands where on the real issues comes when consumers break out of their institutionalized roles, and become producers and administrators. Then the emotional disturbance of those who feer freedom surfaces at once.

Those who deny that 'the only freedom of the slightest importance is the freedom to change one's commitments'[5] and one's roles, are denying the greatest gain made since the Middle Ages. Ironically, the combination of a feudal attitude to social classes with the institutionalization of personal services actually reduces existential freedom – especially in the sphere of everyday activity. The rich of the modern world have made immense gains in social and geographic mobility and they consume enormous quantities of matter. But this has only been achieved thanks to the division of labour and the segregation of classes on a massive world-wide scale, and to the abandonment of local and personal control over the way we feed, clothe and house ourselves.

[5] Sir Geoffrey Vickers in a talk at the Architectural Association Graduate School, London, 5 May, 1975

1

Fig. 1. How many admirers of Brasilia stay there longer than necessary to see the principal buildings and, perhaps, one of the superblocks?

2

Fig. 2. How many designers of places like Brasilia prefer to spend their holidays in places like Mykonos? The escalating prices of 'architecture without architects' largely limit the buyers, and even transient visitors, to those who serve the very organizations that inhibit and destroy what they seek with their earnings. (The writing on the wall over the head of the woman of Mykonos reads 'For Sale.')

ΠΩΛΕΙΤΑΙ

3

16

Fig. 3. The very wealthy can effectively demand costly simulations of traditional forms, as in Port Grimaud, France. (Photo by M. Cooke-Yarborough.)

Fig. 4. Relatively wealthy governments can be persuaded by their advisors to balance social benefits against additional material costs, as in this housing estate in the London Borough of Camden.

4

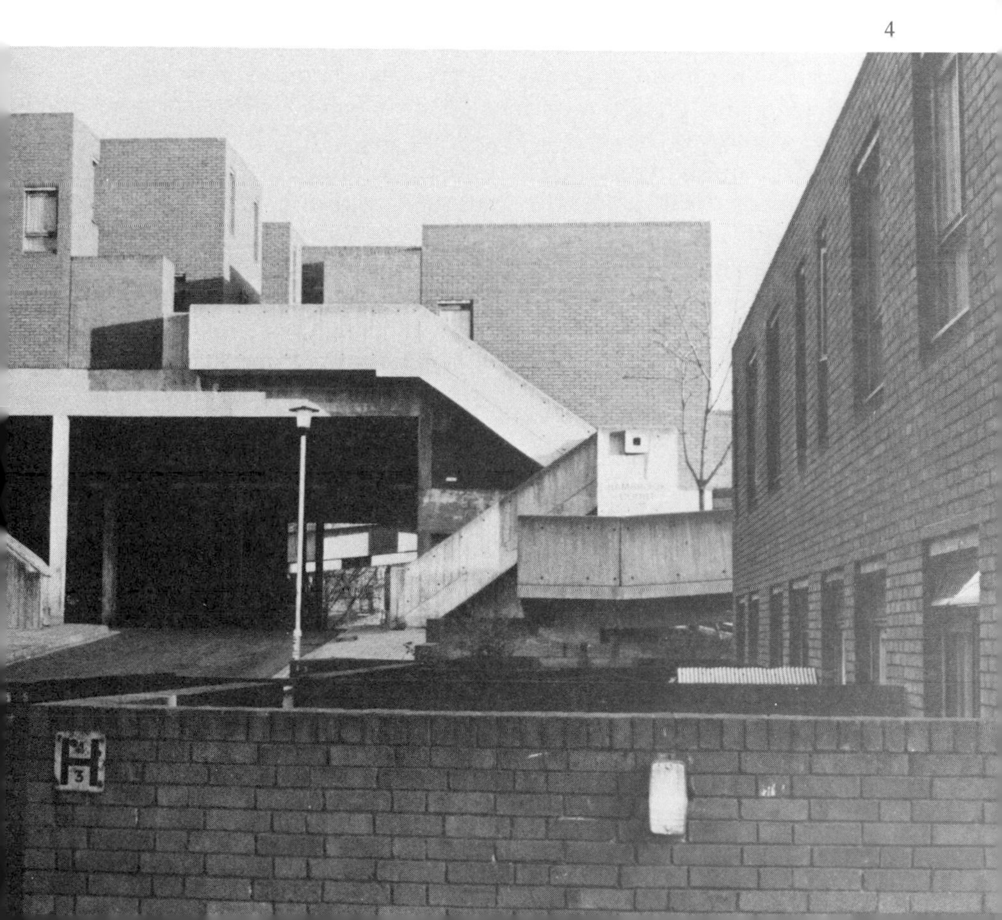

Paternalism and filialism, the modern descendents of attitudes more generally associated by Europeans with the Middle Ages, are still very common attitudes in Britain. These are especially evident in the common assumption that the 'ordinary' citizen or 'layman', is utterly dependent on the 'extraordinary' citizen or the 'professional', who cultivates the mystery of his or her activity in order to increase dependency and professional fees. However, citizens are at last getting wise in rapidly increasing numbers. This has been encouraged by the radicalization and incipient deprofessionalization of the institutionally 'closed shops'. Personal capability is at last resurfacing after the urban-industrial flood.

The most dramatic proof is in the 'upper-lower income countries' of the Third World, such as Greece and Turkey, or Chile and Peru. Examples of what non-professionals can achieve for themselves, are doing much to awaken their wealthy exploiters to the issues discussed here. For some of those in power, this has been a very rude awakening. A friend and an acquaintance of mine were visiting the vast *urbanizaciones populares* of Arequipa Peru (Fig. 5), some time in the mid-1950s. Hernan Bedoya, then director of the regional branch of the national urban planning office (ONPU), was showing the rapidly self-improving squatter settlements to Pedro Beltran, then owner and editor of *La Prensa,* a major national newspaper, and president of the newly formed commission for housing and agricultural reform (and later Minister of Finance and Prime Minister). Almost every plot around them was a building site with permanent structures of white tufa stone, or brick and concrete, under construction; and the area they were visiting was already about five kilometres wide and two deep. Beltran saw a vast shanty town, instead of a huge construction site. Bedoya was speechless when Beltran went on to speak of his determination to rid these poor people of their dreadful slums which were in fact their pride and joy. This incident was echoed when in 1964, on days closely following one another, I took a visiting British Minister of State and a visiting colleague experienced in community development in Africa, to similar settlements in Lima (Fig. 6). Both were profoundly impressed – but in opposite ways. The minister was depressed, the community worker delighted.

It is easy to anticipate how wealthy observers feel when confronted with such overwhelming demonstrations of local actions from which they cannot insulate themselves with misplaced pity.

Very deep changes of attitude have to take place before traditional politicians and 'unreconstructed' professionals can really serve ordinary people as they pretend. This was demonstrated in a remarkable dialogue between representatives of *Nueva Habana* – the well-known Chilean *campamento* shown in the film of that name[6] – and an official of the Allende government. In this perhaps typical case of a people attempting to revolutionize the power structure and change the role of government, the well-meaning administrator was unable to imagine that the people could teach their own children, and that all he had to do was to authorize them and provide a *few* resources – at a vastly lower cost per child than the system which the bureaucrat was hopelessly locked into. The only bureaucratically conceivable role of government is the administration of services to dependent and implicitly ignorant and incapable beneficiaries. And, as the Chileans and Peruvians have done, 'ordinary people' – that is, all of us as citizens – have to slough off the vestiges of cap-touching filialism and demand that those in power help us do what we can do locally for ourselves – by guaranteeing our access to fair shares of available resources – and where essential, by

[6] *Campamento*, a film by Tom Cohen and Richard Pierce, 1973. Dist. in Britain by *The Other Cinema*, London

5

Figs. 5, 6. Examples of what non-professionals, and very low-income people, can achieve for themselves are doing much to awaken their wealthy exploiters to the issues discussed in this essay. For some of those in power, this has been a very rude awakening. A Peruvian politician saw the squatter-builders' site in Arequipa (above) as a slum; a visiting British government minister was depressed by the *barriadas* in Lima (right) .

7

Fig. 7. The progressive development achieved by so many ordinary citizens with such limited resources, typified in the sequence of three dwellings in El Augustino, Lima, reaffirms the author's, and his colleagues', faith in people.

providing complementary infrastructure that cannot be installed locally and that can be provided for all.

Networks and hierarchies

The popularity of the book *Architecture without Architects* and the success of the exhibition it was taken from only demonstrate architects' common preference for architecture that has not been designed by architects. And it is confirmation of the thesis that culture literally comes from the cultivation of the soil[7]. Le Corbusier's notebooks are full of sketches of traditional Mediterranean buildings. Although many architects do make sketches as Le Corbusier did and many planners believe with Doxiadis that genuine culture is a process of refinement from the grass-roots up[8], it is difficult to act on these intuitions or convictions and make even a modest living as an architect.

Although the professional mystification of everyday activities and the related specialized skills are blameworthy, professionals tend to over-blame themselves. It is inverted presumption for them to assume responsibilities that pertain to those that employ them, and to society as a whole. Excessive self-recrimination can paralyze the power to act.

At best, the remorseful activist will abandon the field in which he has most potential power and influence in order to 'change the system' on the false assumption that the system is something apart from the process of building. This, in turn, implies that the supply of buildings, of houses for example, is a function and dependent variable of a political superstructure. The autonomously developed settlements of Lima and Arequipa show that this is something less than a half-truth, whether considered politically or as an incipient

[7] Edward Hyams, *Soil and Civilization*, Thames & Hudson, London, 1952

[8] Constantin Doxiadis, *Architecture in Transition*, Hutchinson, London, 1963

language or culture of building (Fig. 7). The contemporary if fragile dynamism of the awakening people of countries like Chile and Peru, in the shape of its building as well as of its political action, is what attracts so many who would be literal 'architects', and who seize opportunities as long as they haven't paralyzed themselves with guilt or ambition for wealth.

The reason it is so difficult to earn a living as a would-be grass-roots architect is that the only employers (or 'clients' as they are euphemistically called) are large organizations and a very small and rapidly diminishing number of wealthy individuals. And it is the former who cut off the specialist from the people he or she wishes to serve, while the latter are irrelevant except, perhaps, for providing opportunities to experiment.

Where local groups and associations of ordinary citizens have formed to act for themselves – such as the *Associaciones de Padres de Familia Pro-Vivienda* in Peru, or even self-build housing associations in Britain – they are either unaware of the good intentions and potential contributions of planners and architects, or distrustful, or scared off by the fees which their professional associations oblige the architects to charge. So, in almost all countries, the great majority of professionals, in this and most other fields, are tied to centrally administered systems.

The number of professionals large organizations employ is naturally limited and, when they are 'efficient', it is a relatively small number in proportion to the population. And on top of this, the number of professionals who have secure jobs and who are also responsible and creative, tends to be even smaller. In the longer view, this is an alarming prospect and a morally depressing one. Future livelihoods, as well as the freedom to live responsibly and work creatively, are at stake.

To clarify the differences between an institutionalized and a would-be grass roots professional, the decision-making structures in each system must be understood.

The simplest way of doing this in housing is to divide the process of decision-making into three easily recognizable sets of operations:

- planning, or operations that generally precede construction
- construction or building operations,
- the management and maintenance of what is built, necessarily following the greater part of the building operations.

These sets of operations should be distributed between the three common sets of actors that is, those persons, groups, enterprises, or institutions that control the resources for the process itself:

- the users,
- the suppliers,
- the regulators.

For simplicity and brevity, I will distort the model a little by matching these three functional sets of actors with three sectors:

- the popular sector, the users,
- the private commercial sector, the suppliers,
- the public sector or government, the regulators.

By and large in the so-called free market and in mixed economies, these three sectors are clearly distinguishable, even though the former two are almost always treated as a homogenous whole. This convention for seeing the users and the commercial suppliers as one and the same thing – the private sector – is too violent a distortion of the way things actually work. The motives and values of private users, and small producers, are substantially different from most commercial producers or suppliers in a modern society.

Large commercial organizations, or 'growth enterprises' exist to maximize financial returns for third parties, or to perpetuate or expand the organization itself, or all three.

Though profitability is often a major factor in individual householders' or house-seekers' behaviour, use-values generally predominate – just as most small businesses are maintained for the livelihood of those that run them rather than for investors or for the sake of the enterprise as an institution. The public sector, or public agencies, on the other hand, are motivated primarily by the broad political purpose of maintaining their authority over the public order – even though this can be distorted by commercial motives.[9]

The patterns of decision and control describing the two opposite systems are mirror images of one another, as their diagrammatic representation shows. (Figs. 8,9).

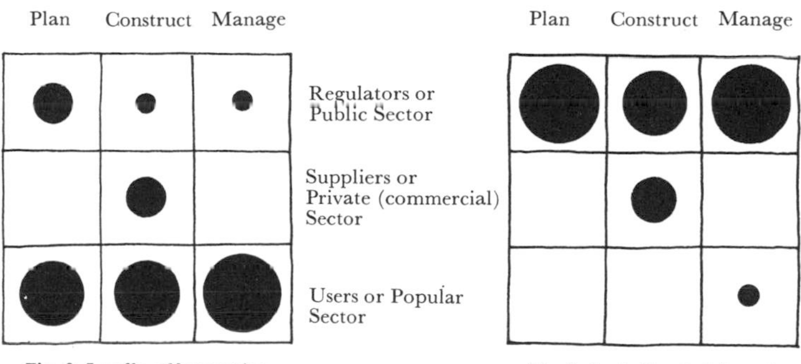

Fig. 8. Locally self-governing or autonomous housing systems.

Fig. 9. Centrally administered or heteronomous housing systems.

The organizations represented by these two patterns are totally different. When both normative or rule-making and operational or gameplaying powers are centralized,

[9]In mixed economies, of course, public enterprises replace some private commercial enterprise and, in planned economies, they are replaced altogether. (In a more sophisticated model, these sectors and the previously described functional groups should be differentiated in order to observe their independent variability).

decisions flow from a peak of authority down through divisions of labour at successive levels to the base. There, whatever is left of the resources funnelled through the system are supplied as categorical goods or services; that is, categories of institutionally designed products are made available to institutionally defined categories of consumers. But when rule-making and game-playing decisions are separated (along with an umpire to complete the democratic principle of separate legislative, executive and judicial powers), an entirely different structure emerges: a non-hierarchic network of autonomous, or semi-autonomous decision-makers, free to combine as they will, as long as they stay within limits set by the rules.

The rules of such democratic games must act as *limits* to action, rather than as prescribed *lines* of action. Those unfamiliar with the vital difference between *pro*scriptive law ('Thou shalt nots') and *pre*scriptive law ('Thou shalts'), and who wrongly suppose that proscriptions limit freedom, should consider the difference between moving between any two positions along railway lines in a marshalling yard which must be followed (Fig 10), and between any two positions along streets in a city which are defined by boundaries which may not be crossed (Fig 11).

This exercise illustrates the principles of equifinality and requisite variety which are essential to freedom and genuine culture, and without which peoples' needs can never by satisfied. Equifinality – a word that has not even made the *OED Supplement* – is the systems-term for the multiplicity of routes to the samc cnd. It emphasizes the often forgotten interdependent variability of ways, means and ends.

To continue the analogy of the railway lines and streets, the former can be used with only one type of vehicle – trains. The latter, on the other hand, can be used by pedestrians, riders of animals, human or animal drawn vehicles, motor vehicles, or bicycles. There are a very limited number of stations in the railway system, but the street user can stop anywhere without blocking the way for others – as long as his vehicle isn't too big in proportion to the traffic flow. And, of course, the number of routes and combinations of routes and vehicles between any two points in each system varies from one in the authoritarian line system to a very large number indeed in the democratic limit system.

The significance of these facts is stated by Ashby's Principle of Requisite Variety: *If stability (of a system) is to be attained, the variety of the controlling system must be at least as great as the variety of the system to be controlled*[10]. In housing, this implies that there must be as large a number of decision-makers, or controllers, as variations demanded for the maintenance of a stable housing system. The coincidence of extreme instability in modern housing systems, *and* their rigidly hierarchic nature, supports this proposition. In Britain, for example, there is a polarization of two dominant systems – the public sector and the private commercial sector. To an increasing extent both are controlled by 'ever-larger pyramidal structures', by a rapidly decreasing number of 'local' authorities in the public sector, and speculative developers in the private, commercial sector. This has already resulted in grossly coarse-grained cities which exclude those who fail to fit the officially or commercially specified categories. The inevitable consequences have been gross misfits and mismatches, and a growing proportion of homelessness.

The high and inevitably spiralling costs of hierarchic systems (as will be explained later) have created a disproportionate dependency on borrowed capital. The result of this has been that the servicing of most homes exceeds the reasonable limits of what most occupiers can pay – and, collectively, the limit of what government can

[10] W. R. Ashby, *Self-regulation and Requisite Variety*, chapter 11 of *Introduction to Cybernatics*, Wiley, 1956, reprinted in *Systems Thinking*, ed. by F. E. Emery, Penguin Modern Management Readings, London, 1969

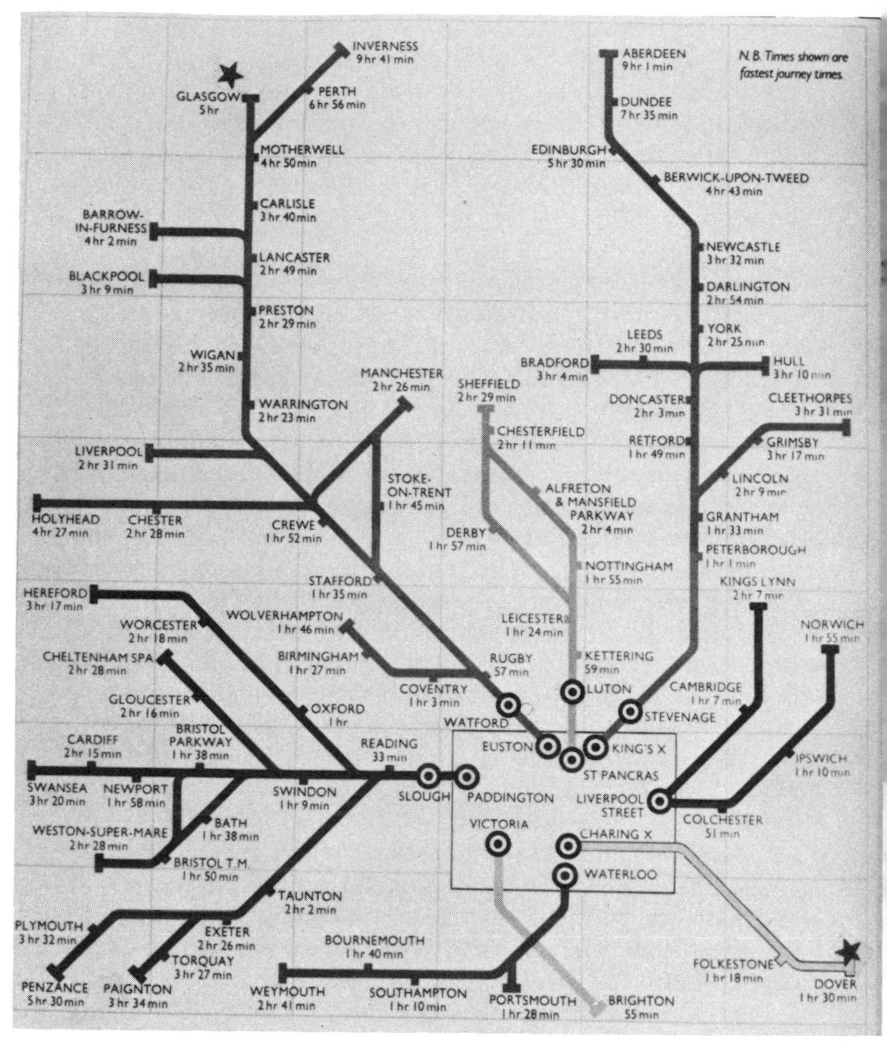

Fig. 10. A hierarchy provides only one route between any two points, as between Glasgow and Dover on this railway map.

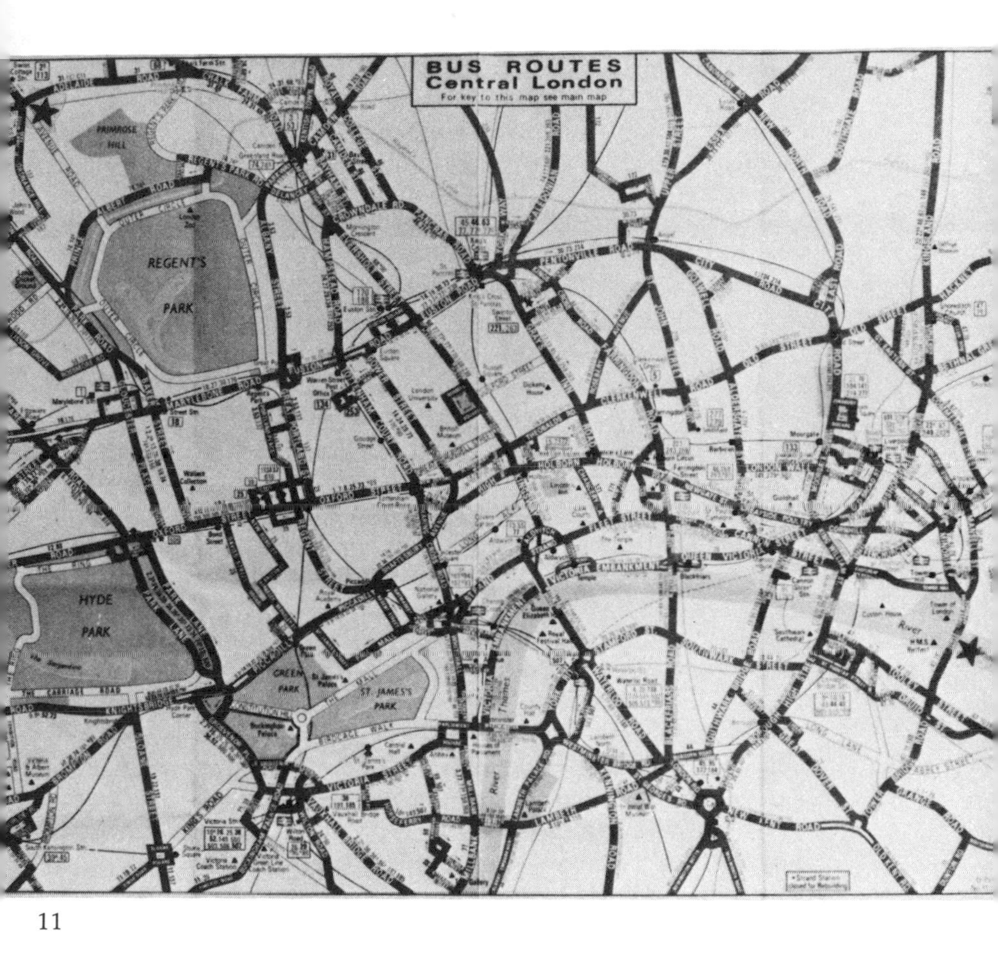

11

Fig. 11. A network, as demonstrated in this London bus-route map, provides a number of routes and combinations of routes between any two points, e.g., between Swiss Cottage and Tower Bridge.

12

Fig. 12. Pruitt-Igoe, an architectural-award-winning public housing project built in St. Louis, Missouri, was partly demolished twenty years later as a result of its unpopularity and vandalization. (Photo by UPI.)

Fig. 13. Fergusleigh Park, Paisley, Scotland: abandoned houses destroyed by 'vandals' forty years after this once popular model public housing estate was built.

afford from national income without upsetting the economy as a whole. (According to recent estimates, British public housing tenants pay 40 per cent of the average costs – and nearly one third of all dwellings in Britain are publicly owned).[11] In planned and market economies alike, these hierarchic systems are collapsing financially, sometimes socially, and even physically. (Figs. 12,13).

Systems generated or maintained by network structures, on the other hand, flourish. They only lose their stability and die as a result of actions or inactions by hierarchic structures whose interests are threatened.

[11] After the above was written, it has been admitted by the London Borough of Camden that average costs of management and maintenance of public housing exceed the average rent of between £6-7 weekly. These and related matters were discussed at a conference on cooperative housing at the Architectural Association, London, February, 1976

Fig. 14. Housing generated and maintained by network structures, in contrast, may flourish indefinitely. This street in Chiddingstone, Kent, has changed little during the last four hundred years.

2. POLLUTION OF RESOURCES

Organizations and the Use of Resources

The previous chapter raised the issue of autonomy versus heteronomy in human settlement and housing in a way that suggested the dependence of both justice and economy on local and personal responsibility and control. The triply polluting consequences of centrally administered or heteronomous systems – the hideousness of characteristic modern housing being the reflection of the defilement of personal relations and the desecration of life, as well as the dirtying of the environment – are inevitable to the extent that they divide and alienate.[1] If decision and control systems governing the supply and use of personal services such as housing must be the primary responsibility of the users in order to generate the 'requisite variety' demanded by Ashby's Law then housing economy and equity can only be achieved if householders and their local communities are responsible for what is built and how it is used and maintained.

This chapter explores the implications of the fact that so many houses over 400 years old, (Fig. 14), are in good condition, while so many less than 40 years old, (Fig. 13), and built at a far greater scarce-resource cost, are already in such poor condition that they have to be demolished. As

[1]I am indebted to Ivan Illich for pointing out the triple meaning of *pollution* in a draft he gave me for a paper entitled Triple Pollution (1971). It subsequently occurred to me that these three perverted relationships relate to the three spheres of life: the relationship between persons; the relationship of (interrelated) persons with their own cultural environment, and of human culture with the larger universe of which it is a (dependent) part.

a commentator remarked while this was being written, the horizons (of British housing) are dark with chickens coming home to roost.

British housing policies, roosting or not, have only been achieved by a relatively equitable distribution of national income. This has been achieved, in turn, thanks to institutional reforms within a system based on the exploitation of other people. People who were once out of sight and out of mind are now separated from us by such rapidly shrinking geographical distances that they can no longer be ignored. This has been resolved by switching (at least in part) from exploiting people to exploiting non-renewable resources and using polluting technologies. These, of course, exploit people separated from us by future time – our own children and grandchildren. The stability of this system of exploitation is being disrupted by ever diminishing returns as the prices of these non-renewable resources inflate with their impending exhaustion. And, not surprisingly, as wealth decreases, so do the opportunities for sharing it out.

This exploitation of people and resources has been reciprocated by an equally hypocritical, and sometimes deliberately subversive exporting of urban-industrial expertise to low income countries. And one would have to be blind not to see how quickly the chickens roost in these poor and inflationary economies. The absurdity of excessively costly, centrally administered supply systems for personal services becomes monstrous in countries where earnings are low and controlled by foreign powers. The fates of Uruguay, Chile, and Argentina – the wealthiest South American countries that were quick to copy European socialized service systems – are alarming precedents. What happens when a population becomes dependent on an institutionalized supply system that can no longer be maintained?

The coincidence of a 60 per cent subsidy of Nonoalco

Tlatelolco, an eleven-thousand dwelling unit publicly-sponsored housing scheme in Mexico City, and the 60+ per cent level of subsidization of local authority housing in Britain, is illustrative. Obviously Mexico cannot possibly provide subsidies of this magnitude for more than a fraction of the population. And in Britain where just management and maintenance costs for public housing often exceed the rents collected, which therefore make no contribution to the annual bill for £3,000 million for the interest charges on public housing debts, it seems highly unlikely that housing can continue to be supplied as a public service.

To treat housing as a commodity is silly enough, but to assume that it must or should be supplied by 'ever-larger pyramidal structures and centralizing technologies' is suicidal. Yet this is the basis of all modern housing policies – a quicksand into which they all sink, even if they can be kept afloat awhile with money. And all this has gone on while real demands have been almost completely ignored or misinterpreted by heteronomous systems impervious and blind to the plentiful resources available.

Mismatches

Forecasts of housing demands always fail. This occurs mainly because it is wrongly supposed that people will spend a given proportion of income on housing. These calculations of what people will spend are based upon what bank or government agency officials assume people can invest. The likelihood of what people *can* and what people *will* spend on housing being similar may be much greater in highly institutionalized contexts such as Britain. But close observations in North and South America and in-depth studies in Central America[2] suggest that apparent

[2] A major source for this essay is the field work carried out in Mexico under Tomasz Sudra's direction. The most important part of his work, based on methods we have developed together from my earlier work in Peru and with students at MIT in Boston, are in-depth case histories of

coincidences of what people *will* spend and what they *can* spend are superficial.

When people are free of the pressures to conform – a freedom people are capable of asserting overnight – the variety in what people will spend is enormous, even within the same income bracket. This is so especially at upper-lower and lower-middle income levels, or at any level at which the household and person is relatively free of social pressures to conform with a rigid norm. For instance, the majority of people with median incomes, especially when they are young, are prepared to consider living in a slum in order to save for marriage, for children, for a home of their own, for school or university expenses, or even for possessions like a car. Alternatively, they may decide to spend far higher proportions of income on a house like the Joneses. The same family may jump from one priority to another at any time.

These variations are extreme in low-income countries like Mexico but they may be far smaller for people with extremely low or extremely high incomes. If a family or household has to spend nearly all its cash income on food in order to keep alive, the proportion it *can* spend on housing is negligible – or even negative after feeding and clothing, and paying for the breadwinner's journey to work. So, of course, they squat, or double up with relatives. And to suppose, as many agencies and statisticians do, that any family can spend up to a quarter, or even a third, of its income on housing, is dangerously wrong in such cases.

At the other extreme, the need to conform may be so important for higher income people that they will spend most of their money on housing – to keep up appearances. Such families, with incomes twenty times as great as the subsistence level of the very poor, often invest half their

people's lives and housing experience. At the time of writing Tomasz Sudra was completing the studies in Mexico for his dissertation at the Department of Urban Studies and Planning at MIT.

income in housing. So, even if the average works out at the officially assumed norm, the variations between investment capacity and priorities are enormous and far too great to ignore the consequent mismatches between housing supply and demand. Until this point is understood, policymakers will continue to be bewildered and exasperated by the apparently arbitrary differences between expected and actual housing behaviour.

These frequently unexpected differences are especially common among lowest income sectors, partly because of the inelasticities just mentioned and also because their priorities are so poorly understood, or so deeply disapproved of, by the high-income legislators, technicians, and administrators who set the rules governing what people may do or get. In low-income and rapidly urbanizing countries, it is unusual for a government agency to recover more than half the payments due from renters or buyers of publicly sponsored housing. Huge publicly financed low-income housing programmes, such as that of the *Banco Obrero of Venezuela* (Figs. 5,6), have been driven to the verge of bankruptcy by such failures. And the photographs of Fergusleigh Park (Fig. 13), vandalized to the point of destruction, and Pruitt-Igoe (Fig. 12) show what can occur in the wealthiest countries.

The imperviousness of large organizations to local and human inputs

The viability of any housing system depends, in the long run, on the efforts of the users and therefore on their *will* to invest those efforts, and not just on their capacity to do so. If that will depends in turn on the level of satisfaction with the service received or expected, then the matching of housing services with their users' priority needs is clearly critical.

It is suggested in this essay, that the components of housing needs are more complex and more variable than allowed by housing law and policy. If this is true, then mismatches between housing supply and demand will be directly proportional to the degree of heteronomy in the system. In other words, the greater the dependence of housing on hierarchic supply systems, the greater the mismatches, the greater the inhibition of users' resources, and the smaller and the poorer the eventual supply. So, the more housing that is provided by centrally administered systems, the bigger will be the gap between potential and actual production, and the worse will become the housing conditions – *immediately* in low income countries, and in *all* contexts in the longer run.

Though generally overlooked, it is self-evident that personal scale and local variety are natural and even inevitable functions of local and personal decisions. Centralized decision-making systems, however, are bound to generate standarized products on a large scale. Of course it is expensive for top-down structures to accommodate bottom-up decisions, or even to copy the forms they generate, and it is equally extravagant for local decision-makers to copy the products of large organizations. What must be recognized here, is that pyramidal structures are impervious to personal and local inputs in proportion to their size.

The reasons hardly need explanation. The larger the organization, the greater the distance of the managers from the shop floor or its equivalent. And even where the workers actually making or delivering the goods can be reached by the users, they are unable to modify what they do without disorganizing the system. There are only two ways of reducing scale and increasing variety and 'personalization' of centrally administered products (and this includes housing) and both demand extra production time – a kind of time that costs a lot of money. Either a larger variety of standard products must be made, stocked, and delivered, or some decisions must be left to those at the lower or lowest levels which, being unpredictable or requiring additional controls, tend to slow the process and anyway demand more administration.

Even if it were possible for a centralized decision and control system to supply the great majority of households with well-matched housing services, their tolerance would shrink, generating even more exacting demands while failing to provide that satisfaction which one gets from having made a decision or having done something for oneself, however imperfect it may be. While people tend to intolerantly look a centrally administered gift horse in the mouth, they show a surprising facility for mulitplying the blessings of something they have done for themselves.

If the observation that heteronomy is impervious to personal and local participation is correct, then to provide variety, centrally administered systems must either relinquish decision making to those who control local resources, or replace organic and human resources with mechanical ones. While acceptance of the former – greater localized autonomous control – weakens the centrally administered system, the excessive use of mechanical means to provide variety pollutes. In either case heteronomous systems for local and personal services are inevitably counter-productive.

In a market economy, heteronomy, because of inherent bureaucracy and waste, is inflationary as soon as scarcities of those resources of which they make extravagent use are perceived, feared or created. And in any kind of economy, dependence on resources limited by scarcity or by counter-productive side effects, will create conflicts of interest between those who possess the resources and those who do not. Further, there will be a conflict between the interests of present and of future generations.

Those with reified values that take centralized administrations for granted and assume that personal, small and local enterprises are intrinsically uneconomic or incompetent, will read this argument as a reaction against all technological and institutional developments since the industrial revolution, and as a call for a return to hard labour for the great majority. This is not the view of those that see how much more effective locally organized systems are for personal services such as housing, and who are therefore sensitive to the vital differences between centralizing and decentralizing technologies and control systems.

Diseconomies and dysfunctions

A brief review of the common characteristics of centrally administered housing will substantiate this proposition. The difficulties and therefore rarity of the participation of users or even local institutions in the planning, construction and management of public housing programmes, needs no further emphasis. The consequences of this lack of participation provide the material for an increasing literature on the alienation experienced by modern housing users.[3] The growth of building organizations and local government – management – and the growth of production systems for housing have an increasing similarity to modern factory and office conditions, where the alienation in work is increasing along with the alienation of use.

Although many on the political left are curiously reluctant to admit or discuss the alienation of labour, Marx's observations of the mid-nineteenth century are equally pertinent today.[4]

As is well known by anyone who has employed or been

[3] Eg: Lee Rainwater, *Behind Ghetto Walls* (a study of the Pruitt Igoe housing project in St. Louis, Missouri), Penguin Books, London 1973. *Vandalism*, ed. by Colin Ward, Architecutral Press, London, 1973, and Van Nostrand, New York, 1973. Petra Griffiths, *Homes Fit for Heroes – a Shelter Report on Council Housing*, Shelter, 86 Strand, London WC2, 1975

[4] E. F. Schumacher quotes an 'early Marx' observation that 'the more useful machines there are, the more useless people there will be'.

employed in small firms, or in jobs *for the users themselves*, responsibility, care, and productivity are generally much greater than in the large and impersonal site, factory or office. Disconcertingly for believers in state socialism, the record of personal responsibility and productivity in private corporations tends to be better, rather than worse, than in public services and nationalized industries.

As well as the alienating and divisive effects of centrally administered housing systems on users and producers alike, the relationships they generate between all concerned and the environment they produce together, also tend to be destructive. There is no need to add to the eloquent messages of the accompanying photographs (Figs 15,17), and to common knowledge of the general standard of modern housing design the world over. It is also well known that the larger the schemes, the worse the average design standards.

Much has been written recently on the common material defects of modern housing which is perhaps best summarized in Alex Gordon's analysis of loose fitness, long life and low energy.[5]

In addition to non-quantifiable and scientifically elusive but aesthetically and emotionally shocking effects of excessive uniformity and size, there are a number of measureable consequences of heteronomy in housing. The standardization and size of developments minimize variety and fit, as already observed. Unfortunately, most over-simple observations emphasize the need for physical flexibility within dwellings or of dwellings. This has led to a great deal of investment in expensive construction systems that allow for internal rearrangements and the expansion and contraction of individual units – a mechanical view of 'loose-fit'.

This investment in heteronomous technologies has

[5] Alex Gordon, *Loose Fit, Low Energy, Long Life*, in RIBA Journal, January, 1974

15

Fig. 15. Between 1950 and 1954, 115 *superbloques* were built in several massive developments in Caracas and its port, La Guaira, Venezuela. The 21 de Abril estate in Caracas is shown here upon completion. (Photo by Banco Obrero, Caracas.)

Fig. 16. Although the *superbloques* were intended to rehouse squatters and eliminate the *ranchos* spreading over many hillsides (see Fig. 32), the increased labour demanded for their construction attracted more migrants than those rehoused. The *ranchos* continued to grow and even the more open spaces in the projects themselves were soon invaded by squatters. The area of 21 de Abril outlined in Fig. 15 is shown here ten years later.

6

proved both expensive and of only marginal benefit. It has done very little in the way of providing for the vital needs of the great majority of people. Their requirements are not measured only by arrangements of rooms and windows, but by the degree of accessibility that they have to their friends and relatives, to their sources of income and to the places where they spend it – all of which demand 'loose-fit'. Large-scale systems have created the most segregated cities the world has ever known.

The life of modern buildings, whether blocks of flats or office blocks, is already notoriously short. Millions have watched the demise of the infamous Pruitt-Igoe public housing project in St. Louis, Missouri (Fig. 12) – partly dynamited by U.S. Army engineers only 20 years after it was built and awarded a prize for good design! This is not an isolated case of public authorities giving up on unmanageable and uneconomic housing estates. Several local authorities in Britain have found that it is easier and cheaper to demolish structures that were well-built less than 40 years ago, than to rehabilitate and modernize them.[6]

In the case of the *superbloque* in Caracas (Figs. 15, 16) built by the Perez Jimenez regime in the 1950s, if it had not been for the very costly programme of community development carried out after the fall of the regime, perhaps all 115 of these monstrous 14-storey buildings would also have had to be pulled down. Before the development of an adequate community infrastructure, they had become

[6] Cases in Britain include the Quarry Hill estate, Leeds; East Hill, Wandsworth, London; and one reported in *The Frightening Cost of Failures*, *Building Design*, 26 March, 1976, concerning two ten-storey blocks in Birkenhead, built in 1958. Only 15% of the original loan on the latter has been paid off and the demolition costs are estimated at £270,000. There are about 100,000 'virtually unlettable postwar council houses' in Britain today according to a housing finance review of the Department of the Environment, reported by Jane Morton in *New Society*, London, 8 April, 1976

scenarios for pitched battles between armed gangs that had taken over the buildings and armoured army units. While these are extreme cases, they indicate the risks and trends when central authority is weakened, and they highlight the well-known problems of management and maintenance of large schemes, structurally sound but where so many residents have become alienated. The life of dwelling structures has more to do with human institutions than building technologies. As Colin Ward points out, most cheap speculatively built semi-detached homes of the 1930s are in better shape than contemporary public housing schemes that were built to far superior specifications.[7]

Gordon's low energy characteristic of viable building is receiving a great deal of current attention. Not only does the relatively short life of large-scale, centrally administered modern housing accelerate the exhaustion of scarce resources, but it uses vastly more. Jean Robert has estimated that the energy used in modern building is three times that used in traditional hand-hewn stone construction[8] – and the latter, of course is vastly longer-lived, even with low levels of maintenance. When one adds the fact that by far the greater part of all energy used in modern building is fossil-fuel based, the implications are starkly clear. Again, some may imagine this is a call back to the body-and-soul-destroying labour of the non-mechanized stone quarry, saw pit, and brickmaker's yard. On the contrary, high energy technologies should be used where they will do the most good. The use of high energy technologies must be limited to where they will maximize those local resources which are plentiful, renewable, or both, instead of wastefully manufacturing, transporting and assembling high energy materials such as concrete and steel. Moreover, indigenous buildings offer enormous energy savings over conventional modern buildings. And

[7] Colin Ward, Tenants Take Over, Architectural Press, London, 1974
[8] During a talk given at the Architectural Association, London, 1974

those who suppose that indigenous houses are inflexible should see how well most traditional structures have responded to the changing needs of generations of users. And as a measure of their desirability, they should note the high prices they fetch.

The necessity of an alternative

Personal and local resources are imagination, initiative, commitment and responsibility, skill and muscle-power; the capability for using specific and often irregular areas of land or locally available materials and tools; the ability to organize enterprises and local institutions; constructive competitiveness and the capacity to co-operate. None of these resources can be used by exogenous or supra-local powers against the will of the people.

The imperviousness of large organizations to local and human inputs – which they often actively suppress – is bound to lead to material diseconomies and social dysfunctions. The illustrated case histories in the following chapters confirm what common sense suggests as soon as the essential differences of organization and energy are recognized: as large organizations cannot respond to the diversity and complexity of personal demands, they must substitute centralized powers for inhibited personal will and effort. Authoritarian power can only be maintained by policing or propaganda and by making people behave like machines, or by substituting machines for people. In practice, of course, all four methods are used although in more 'liberal' modern societies, commercial propaganda and industrial automation are preferred.

Large organizations cannot use personal and local resources without standardizing and dehumanizing them. In more overtly brutal times, this was how the Pharoahs built their monstrous tombs. In modern times, the most apparent forms of brutalization are softened by the use of fossil-fuelled machines – although perhaps as much physical hardship is transferred from the industrialized areas to the 'backward' regions which provide the raw materials which supply the machines and their minders. In any case, the larger the organization the greater its dependence on mechanical energies, whether the machines are powered by muscle or by fossil-fuel.

It is now realized that mineral resources are finite and subject to rapid exhaustion, and that their by-products are poisoning the biosphere and even threaten its balance and the existence of higher forms of life. And now this awareness is complemented by the fact that even the poorest nations and the tiniest minority groups can disrupt the largest organizations and systems so that the balance between photosynthetic and metabolic energies and fossil-fuelled and mechanical energy sources has become critical.

Aesthetically hideous, socially alienating and technically incompetent architecture (Fig. 17) is bound to displace that with traditional values (Fig. 18) when fossil-fuelled heteronomy takes over or, as Siegfried Giedion put it, when mechanization takes command.[9]

In the photographed adjacent cases in Las Palmas in the Canary Islands, the costs of the mechanistic substitute for the traditional development are obvious (Figs. 17, 18). The large block of standardized flats is the 'economic' form for the large developers and building companies. But it does not fit the site. The building has a foundation five stories high and the land itself is poorly used. Not only is it more difficult for the residents to get to their uncomfortable flats, which do not even provide space to hang their washing, but there are fewer of them to the hectare. Not only has the ugly block of inconvenient flats cost vastly more to build, and is vastly more expensive to maintain, but much of that money

[9] Siegfried Giedion, *Mechanization Takes Command*, Oxford University Press, New York, 1948

17

18

Figs. 17, 18. The block of flats (left) is a few hundred feet away from the houses (below). This example from Las Palmas, Canary Islands, supports the proposition that aesthetically hideous, socially alienating and technically incompetent architecture is bound to replace that with traditional values when fossil-fuelled heteronomy takes over.

has gone, and continues to go abroad to pay for oil and investment profits to big city financiers. On the other hand, most of the money spent on the far cheaper, pleasing, adaptable and convenient houses has gone and continues to go to small builders and artisans, and far less money goes to financiers and manufacturers of imported high-energy materials and equipment. Thanks to the freedom which the locally controlled system has given to the people to decide and even to build for themselves, the demand for local labour is maintained and the benefits stay with those who have exercized their own imagination and initiative, skills and responsibility.

3. THE VALUE OF HOUSING

What it does versus what it is

In the first two chapters I argued that the construction and maintenance of adequate housing, at prices people and society can afford, depends on the investment of resources which households themselves control. This argument has been based, in part, on the observation that the willingness of people to invest their energy and initiative and their savings or other material resources depends on the satisfactions they experience or expect as a result.

For large organizations to provide adequate housing, they must standardize procedures and products in order to operate economically. By necessity this conflicts with the local and personal variety of housing priorities which this chapter examines. It will explain how it is that the larger the organization and the more centralized management becomes the more frequent and the greater the mismatches are bound to be between people's housing priorities and the housing they get. As the mismatches increase, so does the users' dissatisfaction. As a result, their investment of local and personal resources decreases and other resources must be found as substitutes. These are generally heavy equipment and complex technologies suitable for centralized organization which they further reinforce. As these demand high proportions of scarce and increasingly costly resources, such as fossil-fuelled technologies and highly paid bureaucracies, financial inflation is inevitable. Any further streamlining of centrally administered housing systems to reduce costs only exacerbates what is becoming a vicious cycle where only the very wealthy or a heavily subsidized minority can expect to be adequately housed.

This and the next two chapters deal with the questions of values and standards, the economies and costs they help to determine, the demands and structure of authority that both generate society's values and economies and that are reinforced by them. These issues and problems are illustrated by the experience of ordinary people in common situations. Similar cases can be found in most contemporary urban contexts and I could have used examples from Ahmedabad or Boston. But the Mexican studies are more detailed and have been selected more rigorously, as well as being from a context that is neither exceptionally rich nor very poor. The case studies are from work-in-progress by Tomasz Sudra at MIT at the time of writing. This work is part of a long-term programme of research we initiated together in 1971.

Twenty-five in-depth case studies of moderate and lower-income households in metropolitan Mexico have been methodically selected from surveys to represent the common range of social situations and physical environments. Some of the poorest dwellings, materially speaking, were clearly the best, socially speaking, and some, but not all of the highest standard dwellings, were the most socially oppressive. One is shown in Fig. 19. The shack was occupied by a young car painter temporarily supporting his wife and small children as a ragpicker. The house (Fig. 20) was occupied by a sick and semi-employed mason, his underemployed wife and their student son. The shack was a highly supportive environment for the car painter's family, while the house was an excessively oppressive environment for the others. This apparent paradox, created by false values and confused language, is a very common one, especially in the majority of low-income countries as well as, and perhaps increasingly, in countries like Britain.

19

Fig. 19. The provisional shack of a car painter's family temporarily dependent on rag-picking in a garbage dump in Mexico City. Being rent-free and close to work, urban facilities and relatives, this materially very poor dwelling actually maximizes the family's opportunities for betterment.

20

Fig. 20. The modern standard house of a semi-employed mason, his unemployed wife and their student son. This materially high-standard dwelling, isolating the family from its sources of livelihood and demanding over half its income for the (subsidized) rent-purchase and utility payments, minimizes opportunities for betterment.

There had been a series of unusually wet seasons in Mexico so that paint drying took too long and the turn-over was too small for the car painter to make a living. In order to keep going, the family had moved in with a *comadre* (God-mother) who gave his family the use of her backyard and the facilities of her own house for as long as they needed it. The *comadre* was a *pepenadora*, or rag-picker, who had been allocated a new house when the shanty town by the dump, in which she and her neighbours and fellow rag-pickers previously lived, was eradicated by the public authorities. As a leader among the *pepenadores*, the *comadre* was able to give the car painter access to the dump from which he was able to make a fair living. The car painter was earning about 900 pesos, or approximately 20 per cent more than the absolute minimum for subsistence – just a little more than what is subsequently referred to as a *subsistence income*.[1]

[1]In the sense used in this essay, a person, family, or household (living in a cash economy) has a *subsistence income* when they must spend between 80 and 90 per cent on food and fuel alone if they are to eat well enough to keep themselves in good health. Close observations in Peru, corroborated by evidence from Mexico and other contexts, suggests that the poorest can often avoid payment for other essentials. Housing can be free through squatting or doubling up with friends or relatives (as in the case described in this chapter) and the journey to work may be made on foot. In many cases, the official 'minimum wage' is roughly the equivalent of a subsistence income for a family of median size in rapidly urbanizing countries (two or three adults and three or four children). As this version of a subsistence income is cross-culturally applicable to urban economies it is a convenient unit of income measurement permitting comparisons between totally different contexts without complicated and often misleading calculations of monetary exchange rates. A growing body of empirical evidence also suggest that there are some widely applicable generalizations with regard to multiples of the subsistence income unit. In Indian, North and East African, as well as South and Central American contexts the income threshold between those who can and cannot afford housing to approved official minimum standards (remarkably similar in remarkably dissimilar countries) appears to be between four and five times the subsistence level as I have defined it. It takes about twice as much (8 to 10 times subsistence) to pay for a standard of living similar to that enjoyed by median income families in highly industrialized and urbanized countries.

Thanks to its rent-free accommodation, the family has a small surplus for saving toward its anticipated move, perhaps towards the purchase of a plot of land and the construction of its own permanent dwelling. The family pays its share of the utilities – its shack is supplied with electricity from the *comadre's* house, and it uses the running water, washing, bathing and toilet facilities. In the relatively mild climate of Mexico City the poorly insulated shack is not too great a hardship as long as the roof keeps the rain out – which it does adequately thanks to the use of plastic and other materials culled from the dump. Together with the use of the enclosed and private backyard, the family has plenty of personal space for its domestic life. It is well located, both for work and social activities. There are shops and schools for the three children in the immediate vicinity, so little or no money has to be spent on transportation. Its security of tenure is invested in the *compadrazgo* (God-parent/God-child) relationship between the car painter and the owner-occupier of the property. As long as this relationship holds, the car-painter's family is secure, and it is rare that such relationships are broken.

The car painter's family is young. It is also optimistic about its future prospects and the couple are confident and self-respecting. Barring accidents and major depressions in the national economy – both of which are quite possible, of course, and are bound to be sources of anxiety – it is very likely that the family will greatly improve its social and economic condition in the course of the car painter's working lifetime.

Being young, healthy and motivated by expectations of future achievements, the car painter household's priorities are well matched by the housing services they have. They therefore need to maximize opportunities for the realization of the family's hopes and expectations, and they make the best use of their surplus – in this case to save as much of their income as possible in order to be able to take advantage of opportunities as they arise. A very common opportunity could be a steady job that would justify investment in a permanent home. This in turn, would provide a substantial degree of security against risks of accident, economic depression or political upheavals. The family's present strategy, therefore, is to minimize housing expenditure. In order to do so, the family must be within walking distance of the earners' places of work and to other essential services. The physical quality of the shelter is secondary and almost anything will do as long as the health of the family is not unduly threatened, especially by contaminated water or exposure to damp and cold. As the family is on the look-out for new job opportunities, which may be in any part of the city or even in other cities, it must be free to move at short notice. Meanwhile, of course, continuity of tenure is important.

All these conditions are met by the car painter's shack. While the family would undoubtedly enjoy a higher standard dwelling this is relatively unimportant. In fact the car painter declined the *comadre's* offer of a room within her house as he did not want to risk damaging their relationship. This materially very poor dwelling was extremely well located for the family at that time; the form of tenancy was ideal, giving them security without commitment and the freedom to move at short notice; and the shelter itself provided all the essentials at minimum cost. The shack was, therefore, an admirable support for their actual situation and a vehicle for the realization of their expectations.

The oppressive house

The mason's modern standard house is disastrously unsatisfactory. Previously resident in a shanty town not far from their present site on the edge of the city, this family had been instrumental in pressing for rehousing when the existence of the shanty town was threatened by the government authorities. Before relocation in the Vicente Guerrero public housing project (Fig. 20) the family supported itself from a small shop serving tourists and from the elderly husband's irregular employment as a semi-skilled mason. The family had a low income but with low housing and transportation expenditures, it was able to eat reasonably well and maintain a fair level of health. Their reported income during the period immediately before the move was about three times the subsistence minimum.

This family now lives in a vastly improved modern house, equipped with basic modern services and conveniences. However, this 'improvement' is endangering the lives of the family members, and in human and economic terms has led to a dangerous deterioration of their condition. Incredibly, the family is required to spend 55 per cent of its total income to meet the rent-purchase and utility payments. On top of this, the working members must pay another 5 per cent for public transportation to work – a total of at least 60 per cent of a reduced income on housing services alone. *Before* the family was spending 5 per cent of a larger income on their housing and journeys to work combined, and they could both eat well and save a proportion of their total income. *Now,* or at the time of the interviews in 1973, it is hard to see how they can survive as long as they maintain their rent-purchase and utility payments. If the assessment of subsistence living costs are approximately correct, this family is now forced to cut down its minimum food budget by about 60 per cent.

This family's situation would not be quite so bad if, in addition to the dramatic rise of their expenditure, they had not also suffered a substantial reduction of their income through the loss of the vending business which is forbidden in their new location. This double loss is typical of 'housing improvement' programmes for low and very low-income people. In spite of the anxieties created by overspending (sometimes on household goods which they feel are appropriate to their new surrounds) or the risks of eviction for rent arrears, people appreciate the comforts of higher standard homes. An unpublished study of rehoused squatters in Rio de Janeiro [2] confirms the common-sense expectation that people like comfort. In the Brazilian case some households that had given up paying rents that they could not afford were actually improving their flats. Laying down a parquet floor, for example, is a way of consolidating *de facto* tenure and a defence against eviction.

But it also confirms that the price paid is often disproportionately high and that much damage is done by dislocating people, by disrupting their economies, and by greatly reducing their social and economic security – far more than by allowing them to remain in materially poor surroundings.

Of course there is a danger that these facts can be used as an argument for laissez-faire. But they can also be used to argue for major changes of government housing and urban development policy. Changes in these conventional redevelopment programmes that appear beneficial but which, by evading the vital issues of building land and housing finance, are in fact instruments of oppression widening the gap between the poor and the rich.

The semi-retired mason's household is an elderly one, in contrast to that of the young car painter's. The mason and his wife were respectively 55 and 54 years old and had one son of 15. Their expectations for the future were low – at best the family could hope to maintain itself at a tolerable, if very low level. The husband was ill and unable to work at the time of the interview. The son was likely to split off and the elderly couple could not rely on their child for much support. Their main priority, therefore, was security. At their previous location in the shanty town – and like the

[2] Barney Rush, *From Favela to Conjunto: The Experience of Squatters Removed to Low-Cost Housing in Rio de Janeiro, Brazil,* Unpublished Paper, Harvard University, 1974

car-painter's family in their present location – the household optimized its budget by minimizing its housing expenditure. In its present (1973) housing situation however, the household is being forced to maximize its housing expenditures – not minimize them. Its budget is not a function of the household's priorities but, rather, of external conditions which are imposing an economic behaviour contrary to the members' interests.

In their previous situation there was a positive match between their priorities and their housing services. The family's housing priorities were naturally for security of tenure and access to their sources of livelihood. As events proved with the clearance of their shanty home, they did not have secure tenure, but they did have immediate access to their main source of income – their stall selling to tourists. The mason had good public transport connections to areas where there was work. The family was also able to economize on housing as they lived rent free and had only to pay for electricity. They were therefore able to maintain their rudimentary but tolerable shack in order. They were able to feed and clothe themselves reasonably well, and most importantly, they could save for security in their old age.

In their present situation they have lost nearly all these advantages and they acquired others of secondary importance. They lost access to a major source of income and as events proved, were unable to maintain the absurdly high level of housing expenditure. This had a two-edged effect: not only were they less secure in their tenure than before, but they were also unable to provide for their approaching old age; and, of course, their food and clothing needs were sacrificed for the benefits of their greatly improved shelter. Whether the family was more comfortable or not, with the anxiety and hunger that they certainly experienced as soon as their savings were used up, is a not-so-open question.[3]

The issue of housing value

If the usefulness of housing for its principal users, the occupiers, is independently variable from the material standards of the goods and services provided as the case studies and other sources show, then conventional measures of housing value can be grossly misleading. As long as it is erroneously assumed that a house of materially higher standard is necessarily a better house, then housing problems will be mis-stated in terms of the number of 'sub-standard' units 'needed' – that is, the difference between the number of households and the number of standard or above standard units occupied at acceptable densities in a given area and period. So long as these assumptions continue, it follows that the solution of such 'problems' is the replacement of sub-standard by standard or above-standard units. The evidence quoted above shows that 'solutions' of this kind can greatly increase the problems suffered by their intended beneficiaries. And this is an increasingly common observation in all contexts from Britain to Brazil where major 'slum clearance' and 'rehousing' schemes have been carried out.

This confusion and consequent error can only be avoided by recognizing the different meanings of 'housing' and 'value' and by using them properly. Market values are, of course, different from human values.

In English the word 'housing' means both the stock of dwelling units (a noun) and the process by which that stock is created and maintained (a verb).[4] It is entirely reasonable to speak about the market value of houses. It is

---

[3]Since the interviews with this family in 1973, the subsidy on cornmeal, the staple diet of the poor, has been withdrawn and the price of *tortillas* and bread doubled overnight. This family is no longer living in Unidad Vicente Guerrero – hopefully they were able to sub-let and re-establish themselves in a situation similar to the one they were moved from with the illicit proceeds.

[4]John F. C. Turner, Housing as a Verb, in *Freedom to Build,* op. cit.

also entirely reasonable to speak about the human and social values of housing action, or housing processes. But it is absurd to mix these sets of terms and their meanings. As the cases show, the performance of housing, ie what it *does* for people is not described by housing standards, ie what it *is*, materially speaking. Yet this linguistic inability to separate process from product and social value from market value is evident in both commercial and bureaucratic language.

Social and institutional processes have many more or less quantifiable aspects; but, considered as understandable wholes, they are only partly quantifiable. Monetary or market values cannot be placed on them. And it is a disturbing sign of the decay of language and values in the modern world that official housing, building and planning terminology universally confuses the meanings of housing and of housing value.

It seems that all national and international housing and planning agencies mis-state housing problems by applying quantitative measures to non- or only partly quantifiable realities. Only in an impossible world of limitless resources and perfect justice – where people could have their cake and eat it too – could there be a coincidence of material and human values. For the present we must accept that as long as there are unsatisfied desires for material goods and services people must choose *between* the cakes they can afford to eat. So long as this fact of life remains, and as long as people's priorities vary, the usefulness of things will vary independently of their material standard or monetary value.

The vast majority of officials and professionals keep recommending the destruction of people's homes in order to solve those same people's 'housing problems' by providing them with alternatives either they or society cannot afford. In a world of grossly maldistributed resources and injustice, this is a huge, but very black joke.

Such stupidities are inevitable as long as those who perpetuate them have confused their values and lost their common sense of life's wholeness.

Housing problems restated

Georges Bernanos wrote that there is no greater evil than a problem mis-stated. Problems cannot be properly stated, however, unless the underlying issues are understood. All the evidence presented in this book is to show that housing problems can be restated in the light of human values that must be placed on housing processes. Together, they provide entirely reasonable interpretations and indicate actions that are both feasible and desirable for all concerned with well-being.

The real questions are those of human suffering and pollution, as they are directly associated with dwellings, their provision, and their management. Quantitative methods cannot describe the relationships between things, people and nature – which is just where experience and human values lie. They may be essential for determining resource allocation, and as aids in identifying complex systems and their components, but quantitative methods can only indicate, not measure, non-quantifiable components – the human realities of housing. Only by standing Lord Kelvin's dictum on its head can one make sense of it: nothing of real value is measurable.

Questions about the consequences of housing in people's lives can only be asked in words that describe processes and relationships. Housing must, therefore, be used as a verb rather than as a noun – as a process that subsumes products. Real values are those that lie in the relationships *between* the elements of housing action – between the actors, their activities and their achievements.

I use an adaptation of Patrick Geddes' (1877) and Bertalanffy's (1948) general systems models as basic descriptors of any particular housing process in its context

– as a subsystem of the larger system or systems of which it can been seen as a part. Any subject matter of value must have three elements: people, the things they do, and the relationships between the two. Or, as Geddes expressed it: *organism* – *function* – *environment* (where function is the relationship and both organism and environment are acting on each other). In the simplest useful terms, any specific housing process can be described as the interaction of the people (or *actors*) and their products (or *achievements*) through the medium of their roles and responsibilities (or *activities*.) As any such process must take place in a larger context in which the actors live (and have a multiplicity of other and independently variable relationships), and in which their achievements exist, there are three other elements: the pre-existant *context*, the subsequently *modified context*, and the direct relationships between them which by-pass the particular process. Bertalanffy's simplified general systems model recognizes these direct relationships or feed-backs (and feed-forwards). In housing these are the actors' future *expectations* from their past *experience*. Following Bertalanffy, these basic terms can be conveniently arranged thus (Fig. 21).

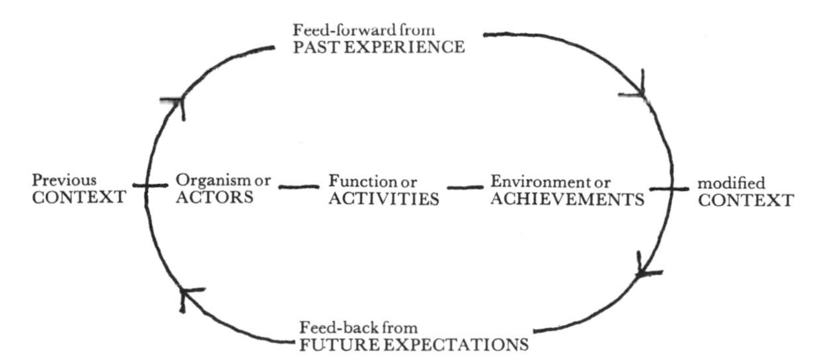

On the understanding that the actors' or decisionmakers' will and their reasons are functions of their past experience and future expectations, the model may be stated as the following composite question: *Under what circumstances, will who do what, why and with what consequences?*

Fig. 21. A simplified model for the housing process based on Geddes and Bertalanffy.

It should be noted, however, that time does not flow from left to right so much as from the bottom up. Although there is a temporal sequence from existing to modified context, the three elements of the subject coexist and contextual modifications occur the moment an action is conceived.

Housing problems only arise when housing processes, that is housing goods and services and the ways and means by which they are provided, cease to be vehicles for the fulfilment of their users' lives and hopes. As the cases described above show, this may have nothing to do with the relative material standard of dwellings. To be of any positive and constructive use, housing problems must be restated in terms that indicate burdens or barriers created by housing procedures, goods and services; or in terms of waste resulting from the failure to use available resources, or the misuse and non-use of resources.

Values, measurement and indicators

'To undertake to measure the immeasurable is absurd and constitutes but an elaborate method of moving from preconceived notions to foregone conclusions.'[5]

Those who agree with Schumacher and reject the preconceived notions on which statistically defined 'housing problems' are based, and who therefore reject the conventionally foregone conclusion that houses of higher material standard are necessarily better than those with lower ones, must find an appropriate way of stating the problem.

The notion of quantifiable measures for human use values must be replaced by matching individual needs with housing – that is, procedures, goods, and services. As pointed out above, and as experienced by everyone who has to make a personal housing decision, the vital matches have to do with location and access to people and places, with tenancy and transferability, and with privacy and comfort.

[5] E. F. Schumacher, *Small is Beautiful*, Blond & Briggs, London, 1974

Only the last item can be easily quantified and then the information can be grossly misleading, as already shown. Even if it were possible to quantify all these factors, it would be a useless exercise because one's priorities vary, often considerably and very rapidly, as one's situation changes. The quantities of houses, or forms of tenure, or even locations, tell us very little about the problems that households actually experience. If one already has a clear idea of the pattern of priorities in a given situation then, of course, these facts can be valuable *indicators*. They can point to the values of specific sets of housing procedures, goods and services, but they will not describe or measure them.

The obvious fact that use values cannot be quantified worries those who assume that housing can only be satisfactorily supplied by large-scale organizations. The immeasurability of use values is not in the least perturbing to the conventional capitalist. His value system can only admit the existence of market values in the sphere of commercial production, distribution and consumption. If what is good for General Motors is good for the country, then it must also be good for the citizen. The conventional socialist, on the other hand, has always been perturbed by the conflict of use and market values – and the more he or she clings to a faith in large organizations (and centralizing technologies) the greater the conflict becomes. On the other hand those who do not believe that large organizations can supply all people with personal goods and services, those who have neither a capitalistic nor an authoritarian outlook, need find no conflict or paradox. Material quantities and market values can be useful, even essential, *indicators* of use value, or of harmonies and tensions between supply and demand. But this principle can only be of use to those who see that the role of central administrations must be limited to ensuring personal and local access to essential resources – such as, in the case of housing, appropriate technologies, land and credit.

In other words, to state the problem of housing (or of any other personal and necessarily local service) depends on who needs the statement and what it is used for.

If housing is treated as a mass-produced consumer product, human use values must be substituted for material values. Whether these are capitalistic market values or state socialist productivity values is immaterial. Both inevitably inhibit the investment of personal and local resources on which the housing supply itself ultimately depends – as explained in the first two chapters. However sensitive individuals in such heteronomous systems may be, they are locked into positions in which this contradiction is inescapable. But if housing problem statements are needed by planners and administrators of non-authoritarian and genuinely socialist societies, then their purposes are quite different. There is no inherent contradiction between the planners, needs and those of the people they serve.

As already pointed out and as will be explained more fully later, in a democratic and genuinely socialist context planning and administration are legislative processes limited to actions essential to establish and maintain an equitable distribution of resources. For centrally administered heteronomous societies, the quantitative information needed for such distribution is extremely complex, but in the case of non-authoritarian societies, the quantitative information needed is quite different and far simpler. All that the latter's central planners need to know is the pent-up demand for *resources* and large-scale *infrastructure* (public utilities and community facilities) which cannot be provided at local levels. Instead of needing to know how many houses are or will be demanded in a given place and time or for a given social sector the planners and administrators need only know the approximate quantities of building materials, tools and labour, land and credit that will be required. So long as the rules within which building, management and maintenance take place ensure tolerable economy and justice, the local forms of these elements can be left to the people and the local entrepreneurs that serve them.

It is an unproven assertion that the problems which people actually suffer from – distortions of their household economies, social and geographic dislocations, insecurities of tenure or immobility, and discomfort and the lack of privacy – can be indicated by ratios and proportions of quantifiable factors. It is more of a working hypothesis, derived from my own studies in Peru in the sixties, and those Tomasz Sudra and I have been carrying out in Mexico for the past few years. We have tentatively concluded that two sets of factors are needed: a financially quantifiable set, and another which cannot be given monetary values with any consistency or comparability.

Monetary factors

On the financial side, the significant factors are: personal household *income* in relation to the *price* paid (for rent or amortization and other running costs); the *cost* to the suppliers of the services provided (of land, buildings and their servicing), and the *assets* owned by the occupants. In a 'planned economy' there is supposed to be no such thing as 'market value' or assets in the form of 'equity' – the share of that value accruing to the owner-occupiers after paying off mortgages or other liens. But, in most cases, there is a market in personal property, including houses – whether officially recognized or not.

The car-painter family's supportive shack shows a positive balance (Fig. 22b); the negligible price paid (a small contribution to his *comadre* as a share of utilities) is a positive imbalance with the household income – indicating, of course, a cost and possible imbalance for someone else, in this case, the *comadre* whose yard the shack is occupying

Comparative Evaluations
The windmill diagrams show the balances and trade-offs, and the imbalances and stresses between the principal housing values in the case histories used to illustrate the argument.

One set (22b-f) shows the patterns of monetary values and the other (23b-f) shows the non-monetary value patterns. By separating these accounts and by highlighting the ratios and proportions of key values, the arbitrariness and distortions of conventional cost/benefit analysis are reduced.

Each sail represents a value scaled in 5 intervals, from a very low value (A) to a very high value (E) through low (B), moderate (C), and high (D). Although these are given quantitative measures they are only approximate in most cases. The most significant information is in the patterns and especially in the matches and mismatches between the actual supply (shown solid) and the households' needs, priorities, or expectations (shown in outline).

Positive, negative and mixed values of these mismatches are indicated by the corresponding signs. Mixed (±) values indicate positive for one sector and negative for another or others. Summary explanations are given in the captions.

Fig. 22a/23a

O = Zero

A = Very low

B = Low

C = Moderate

D = High

E = Very high

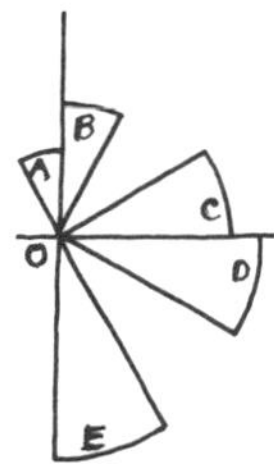

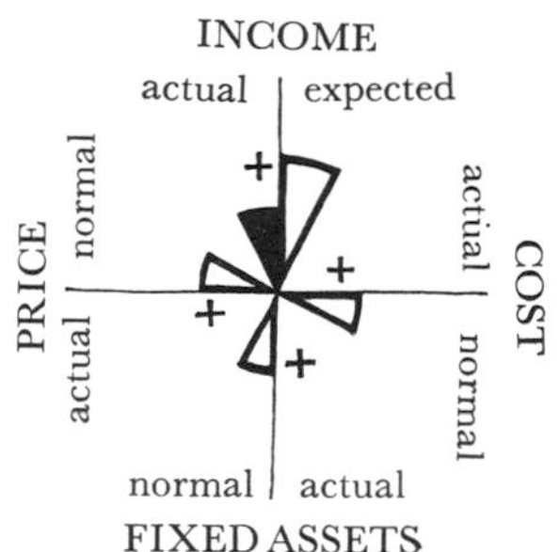

22b: The car painter minimizes costs by living temporarily in a shack in order to maximize savings and future opportunities to realize expectations. The lack of fixed assets ensures mobility and is therefore positive in this case.

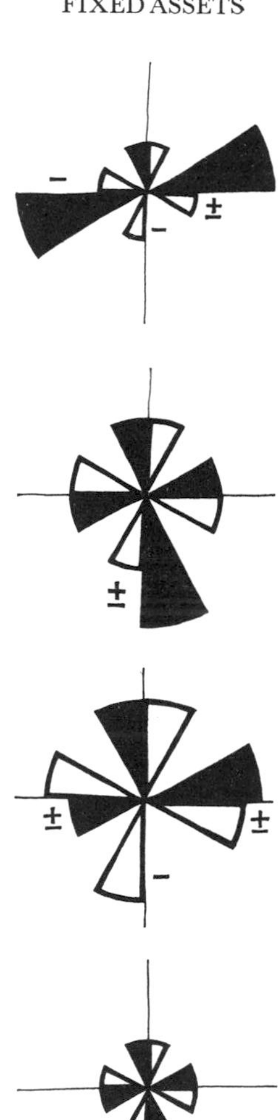

22c: The mason relocated from a squatter settlement to a project suffers the consequences of an extreme mismatch of price and cost with income. There is no compensation in the form of equity although, as he and his wife are elderly, the security of a fixed asset is important.

22d: The factory worker in the progressively developing unauthorized settlement has a balanced housing economy with the advantage of disproportionately high assets. This reflection of inflated land prices is a cost to society as a whole.

22e: The employee in the same project as the mason (22c) enjoys highly subsidized housing for which he is able to pay the economic price, unlike his neighbour. He benefits at society's expense. The lack of equity is temporary and relatively unimportant as income is relatively high and secure.

22f: The vendor, Mama Elena, has a well matched housing economy with exceptionally high assets like the factory worker (22d). As the land is squatted its value is less distorted by inflated market values.

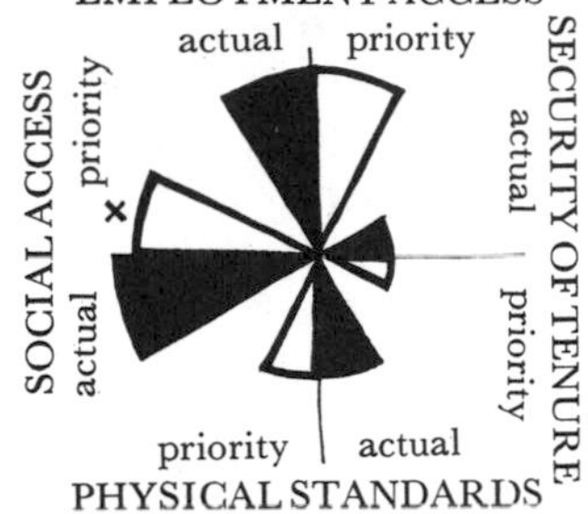

23b: The car painter maximizes access to sources of social and economic support at the expense of comfort and security of tenure. Priorities are well matched. The poverty of the shack is partially compensated by access to utilities.

23c: The mason suffers from extreme mismatches on this side as well as in the monetary account. The family's highest priorities are unmet while their lowest is greatly exceeded.

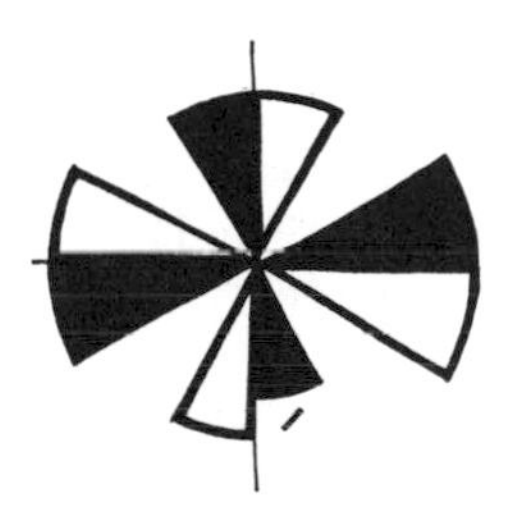

23d: The factory worker has a very well balanced housing performance. The highest priorities for social access and secure tenure are met and the only imbalance, a somewhat lower than desirable standard, is temporary.

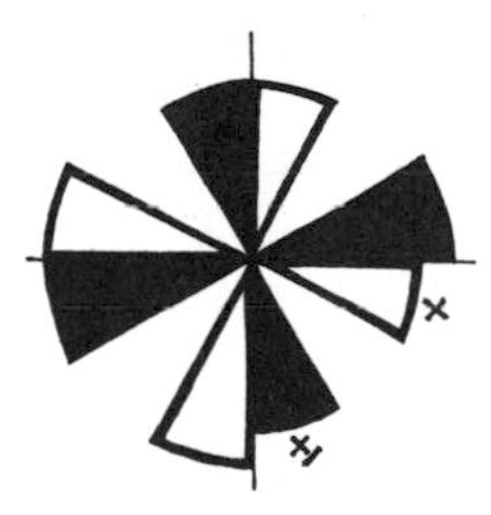

23e: The employee has a well matched housing performance with positive mismatches for the family for shelter and tenure. The former is at society's expense as shown in 22e.

23f: The vendor, Mama Elena, has a well matched housing performance in which all priorities are met with the partial exception of security of tenure. This will be consolidated when the present de facto tenure is legalized.

22a *Key to Monetary Accounts*

INCOME: average total household in multiples of subsistence minimum (S) from below $1\frac{1}{2}$S to above 10S. A subsistence income is that which leaves about 15% margin after purchase of minimum food and fuel.

PRICE: rent or amortization, property taxes, utilities and maintenance paid by household. As % of income from below 5% to over 30%.

COST: construction or replacement cost to supplier whether owner-occupier, developer or landlord. From less than one year's household income to over 5 years' income.

FIXEDASSETS: equity owned by household or key money obtainable. From less than 1 year's income to over 5 years', as above.

23a. *Key to Non-monetary Accounts*

SOCIAL ACCESS: dwelling location as a function of proximity to people on whom the household is dependent for social support. From next door to over 1 day's return journey.

ECONOMIC ACCESS: dwelling location as a function of proximity to sources of the household's income. From the same street to over 2 hours' commute by public transport.

PHYSICAL STANDARDS: space, construction and equipment standards from unsheltered and unserviced to sheltered and serviced to modern minimum standards.

TENURE SECURITY the duration of the household's option for continuous residence. From less than 1 month to more than a lifetime.

rent-free. The cost of erecting the shack was also negligible, so price and cost are in balance – no-one gains or loses. There is no market value as the car-painter cannot sell the shack to anyone (and would hardly get any cash from the sale of the materials even, given the proximity of the garbage dump from whence they came) so there is no equity or assets. One might read a negative imbalance between the household's income and the lack of housing equity; but, in fact, the household is saving in cash and has therefore transferred its potential equity to its savings account. If we knew how much they had stashed away we could indicate that – but this information is rarely available, for obvious reasons.

The unemployed mason family's oppressive house shows an extremely negative balance (Fig. 22c) they pay a price out of all proportion to their income. Even so, there is still a positive imbalance in the occupants' favour between the price (rent-purchase) they pay and the cost to the government for providing the house and its services, indicating a relatively high cost in public subsidies on top of the high cost to the family itself. The family has no equity, as virtually all their payments are for interest in the early years of the mortgage, and they are not free to sell on the open market and cannot transfer.

Non-monetary factors

Equally positive and negative balances are shown up when the non-monetary account is assembled (Fig. 23). This is made up of factors indicating relative *accessibility* (both geographic and social); relative *security* of tenure (both continuity and transferability); and relative physical *standards* (both for the dwelling and its surrounding). It should be noted that the conventional measure of housing problems – the physical standard of the building and its equipment – is but one of eight factors observed and analyzed in this account.

Of course these factors are difficult to quantify, but Sudra and I maintain that it can be done, and done more easily than in the orthodox methods of surveying housing conditions, through the proper selection of a small sample of case studies.

From the above descriptions it is clear that in the car-painter's supportive shack, the accessibility, tenancy, and comfort levels provided match the household's priorities admirably (Fig. 23b). The family has excellent access to their sources of livelihood and the people and services on which its domestic life depends; its insecure tenure suits its temporary status, and the relatively low physical standards are matched by a relatively low priority in this respect.

The mason's family's house, however, is largely negative in the non-monetary as well as in the financial account (Fig. 23c): the project is very poorly located in relation to workplaces, and is poorly equipped with community facilities. The family has also been separated from many of its former neighbours. Its tenancy is extremely insecure as the family cannot maintain the excessively high payments for long, and they cannot legally transfer or exchange it for a viable alternative. They enjoy the increased comfort, but they are paying with their personal health – for their greatly improved physical conditions cost so much of their income that they cannot properly feed and clothe themselves – in spite of the substantial public subsidy.

The problems people actually experience, personally or collectively, are those revealed by these imbalances: poor value for money, financial and social insecurity, isolation and dislocation, and, of course, the bodily and mental hardships of poor physical conditions and lack of privacy.

How much people suffer from such imbalances depends, however, on their actual situations and future expectations. As the examples show, people's priorities vary as widely as their incomes and future outlooks vary. It should now be obvious that no conceivable authority could possibly anticipate the immense variety of household situations, priorities and specific housing needs. The huge efforts and sums spent on surveying housing conditions without reference to people's situations and priorities and without any clear understanding of the housing process, has done, and can only continue to do, a great deal of harm. It is not too much to say that these generally well-intentioned surveys and analyses have merely aided and abetted the destruction of urban communities, painfully built up by generations of people.

There is then, an argument for the redefinition of housing problems as functions of mismatches between people's socio-economic and cultural situations and their housing processes and products; and as functions of the waste, misuse, or non-use of resources available for housing. If this argument is accepted, then major re-orientations of policy must follow. If housing problems are not to be stated in terms of standard unit deficits, housing solutions can no longer be proposed in terms of unit production or productivity. Instead monetarily quantitative housing policy goals will have to be formulated in terms of redressing imbalances between incomes and prices, prices and costs, and costs and incomes. In non-monetary terms, policy goals will have to be reorientated towards the elimination of residential dislocation, insecurity of tenure, and housing-related psychosomatic disease.

4. HOUSING ECONOMIES

Resourcefulness versus productivity

In the last chapter I discussed the paradox of the car painter's shack made from scrap materials and the mason's minimum standard modern housing project unit. While the shack suited the needs of the car painter's family, the modern minimum unit was extremely oppressive for the mason's family. Despite all the mason's modern conveniences, the very poor shanty was clearly a better dwelling. This is the paradox in low-income housing of use-values versus material values. This chapter continues the discussion, using two case studies – a factory worker and a government employee – obtained by Tomasz Sudra in the course of our work in Mexico.

The case of the car painter and the mason is not a special one. The lower-income factory worker's owner-built dwelling (Fig. 24), in an unauthorized 'progressive development' (Fig. 25), is worth a great deal more to his family than the middle-income government employee's project unit is to his. The latter's house is of the same type and in the same housing project Unidad Vicente Guerrero as the mason's home (Fig. 20). And, as the following analysis will show, in a few years' time, the poorer man's house will be worth considerably more than the other's.

Our study of 25 representative cases in metropolitan Mexico revealed that the value of the larger dwellings of the lower-income group averaged more than those built by the higher income renters, whose incomes were up to three times larger than the lower income group. The contrast between rents paid by above median and below median income tenants is even more startling: low-income

24

Figs. 24, 25. A factory worker building a house (above) on a plot bought illegally on the outskirts of Mexico City (right). This low-income worker's unsubsidized self-built dwelling will soon be larger and worth more than standard houses in publicly subsidized projects, most of which are allocated to families with higher incomes.

households have to pay substantially more than they can afford (up to fifty per cent of their income) for their very poor housing, while moderate-income households *underspend* on rents. In fact, a high proportion of the relatively well-off households spent less than five per cent of their incomes on their housing. This appalling discrepancy is relatively common in rapidly urbanizing countries with housing policies copied from wealthy urban-industrial countries.

The conditions described here have their roots in false or misapplied values. As pointed out in the last chapter, it is common for public agencies to build houses or flats to standards which the majority cannot afford, nor can the country possibly subsidize them on a large scale. On top of this, it is not unusual for governments to prohibit private building of the type of housing the vast majority can afford and are satisfied with.

The factory worker

The factory worker's young family is building its own home on a plot bought illegally from an *ejido* – a once rural community that was granted the usufruct of the rough pasture land in perpetuity by a post-revolutionary government (purchasers' *de facto* tenure has since been legalized). So far, they have built a two-room dwelling (Fig. 24) on their 120 square metres and a rather steeply sloping plot on which they also have a laundry and washing area, a latrine and a pigsty. Water still has to be bought from municipal tankers and electricity is obtained from a clandestine shared connection to a low-tension line about a kilometre away.

The total cost of house and plot is the equivalent of three and a half months' income, and their monthly housing expenditure at the time of the interview in 1973 was one sixth of the factory worker's wage, the household's only income. This was mainly for instalments on the land and these would have been completed a year later. Then all the family will have to pay is the cost of water delivery, an authorized supply of electricity, and a small land tax, so their minimum housing expenditure will be about five per cent of their income.

The factory worker's income was typical for most of the metropolitan population – twice the absolute minimum needed by an average family for its food and cooking fuel budget. The market value of the property was the equivalent of about 14 years' present income, but this is largely due to the 30 to 40 per cent annual inflation of land prices. Under more stable price conditions, the value would have still amounted to about three or four years' income. The family intended to add a shop and eventually improve and enlarge their present dwelling. Most likely it will be converted into a two-storey duplex.

The second unit is intended for a second generation family, or for rent – in either case providing the parents with some security and income in addition to the shop already planned. Except for short-term loans, such as the one the factory worker obtained from his employer to buy the land and materials, it is unlikely that any other or more formal kinds of credit will be used or sought. Since the most important priority is for their present and future security, no mortgages would be accepted (a loan from an employer is a guarantee of continued employment, at least until the debt is repaid).

With a steady job and little prospect of future improvement, the growing family had a very high priority for home-ownership and the security that it would provide.

Unlike the car painter, the factory worker was no longer hoping for better jobs and therefore was not giving first priority to opportunities of finding them. He was ready to settle, consolidate and improve his family's status.

The government employee

The government employee, 56 years old when

interviewed in 1973, was born in Tepito, a deteriorated neighbourhood in the central city and famous for its urban folk culture. He and his 40 year old wife and eight children all live in the new housing project.

They were moved to the project after protesting to the President against the redevelopment plan for their old neighbourhood. The government employee, a member of the ruling political party, was among the delegates who got to see the President's wife, who had arranged for them to be transferred to their new homes in Vicente Guerrero.

The employee had had well paid jobs most of his life (and for a time, his own business), and eventually got a good job in a government agency with a salary bordering on middle-income, twice that of the factory worker. Together with the irregular contributions of the two eldest daughters, the household income averaged around five times the subsistence income. Their new house is similar to that of the semi-employed mason whose income was below subsistence level (more than half of which went to pay for the house and utilities). The government employee's family spent only a little more than 10 per cent of their household budget for the rent-purchase, insurance, and utility payments of their house, which would be amortized after 15 years.

The house itself has only 48 square metres of roofed space on a plot of 72 square metres. Nevertheless, it is substantially larger than their previous dwelling which had only 24 square metres – one room and a kitchen-cum-hall space. Compared to the factory worker's house, the government employee's house and land was much smaller. However, as the employee's family was born into very high-density conditions, they were quite content with the space available.

For several years the government employee's family will have very little equity and cannot legally sell on the open market until the property has been amortized. The conditions of sale and regulations governing the uses of the dwelling are, in fact, very limiting and typical of rented public housing in Britain: occupiers are prohibited from using their dwellings for any purpose other than for their own domestic residence. The government employee reported that the neighbour who had painted his house has had to repaint it the original colour – occupiers are even supposed to get permission to decorate their own interiors. Of course, alterations or additions are out of the question, although it is more likely that all these rules and regulations will be forgotten once the project's present status as a showcase scheme has declined (there are few such developments in Latin America in which the majority of houses have not been radically altered within a decade of occupation) (See Figs 38 & 39).

The estimated free market value of the government employee's house was about 45,000 pesos in 1973, or only little over his household's income for one year. The family could easily have afforded commmercially built housing then available, but it would have been unsubsidized and would have cost twice as much. This difference between the subsidized and the market price represents a potential equity, to be realized in the form of key money should clandestine tenancy transfers become as easy to make as they are in most other projects of this kind.

While the project dwelling would not have suited the factory worker's family and budget at all, it was highly acceptable to the government employee and his wife. He was fully insured against even temporary periods of unemployment due to illness. He was unlikely to be affected by strikes or social unrest, and he would soon retire with a good pension with important fringe benefits such as free medical services for his dependants as well as for himself.

Unlike the factory worker, the government employee was not especially concerned with the freehold of his dwelling as there was little or no danger of his being unable to maintain the monthly payments. Although irritated by the rule against businesses in the houses, the family had no need of one, as in the case of the mason and his wife who had had a successful trade in their previous location.

A comparative evaluation

If the four cases described so far – the car painter, the mason, the factory worker and the government employee – are compared in the manner described, (Fig. 22), then a wide range of housing economies is indicated, each representing a significantly different distribution of material costs and benefits to the users, the private commercial sector, and the publicly subsidized sector.

The car painter's squatter shack, for example, has virtually no housing expenses at all, (Fig. 22b). Therefore the household's very low income can be spent on the most important thing of all – food. Any balance can be saved towards their future home. And the only imbalance, the lack of assets, is compensated for by the savings made possible by the rents and cost-free solution to the family's housing problem.

As to the mason's project house, there is a serious economic imbalance. (Fig 22c). The household's budget is intolerably distorted by the excessive price (amortization and running costs) necessary just to keep the house. To maintain these payments, the family's food budget has been cut back to below subsistence level. As the government funded the capital outlay to build the house, no asset can be realized by the mason through relinquishing the house. This outlay of government capital from its very limited reserves, while vastly improving the dwelling conditions of one family, has greatly reduced the opportunities for partially improving the conditions for many more. Further, it has reduced that one family to a below subsistence standard of living – a condition it had not suffered from during its less salubrious shanty town days.

The factory worker's progressive development house is a positively balanced housing economy. (Fig. 22d). Cost (capital outlay) and price (amortization and running costs) are balanced against income, and the assets the family have are substantially greater than the norm. This positive imbalance has increased the household's economic security and social stability. This would be so even if the estimate was based on a normal rise in land values rather than the hopefully temporary gross inflation of current land prices.

The government employee's project housing economy, like the mason's, is also imbalanced (Fig.22e), but with a difference. The government employee's family is paying a price substantially less than they could afford. Although this housing economy offers no assets for the family (at least not for some years) and as such does not contribute to their economic security, home ownership and equity was not a high priority to this family. Their security exists because a large portion of their income is surplus to their subsistence needs, made possible because the housing project is a heavily subsidized government-financed show-case – hardly an equitable or practical allocation of government funds.

Criteria for housing economy

These simplified analyses show that imbalances can be positive as well as negative, and that they may be both at the same time – that is, positive for one sector, and negative for another. Until a great deal of empirical evidence has been accumulated and verifiable formulae are available, it seems unlikely that these patterns can be used as *measures* of economic problems in housing. As *indicators,* however, these patterns are infinitely better than the simplistic and dangerously misleading method of housing standards universally employed by housing policy-makers.

Fewer risks will be taken, and less damage done, if housing problems are generalized from the observation of these patterns of housing economy. The extent to which price (housing amortization and running costs) can be lowered in relation to cost (capital outlay) is then a function of subsidies and the funds available. The lower the national budget per capita, the smaller the feasible imbalance if larger numbers are to be subsidized. The interpretation placed on the ratios of incomes to household assets will be influenced by ideological views on private property. The most commonly expressed prejudice against home ownership in Britain, for example, is that of middle-class intellectuals most of whom are themselves owner-occupiers. Ironically, most socialist states practise the Marxist distinction between personal and collective property. Some East European countries, such as Bulgaria, have even higher ratios of home ownership than the current 53 per cent in Britain.[1] Except for the surviving advocates of collectivized housing, most observers will agree that personally (or co-operatively) owned assets giving households a stake in the physical environment, are essential for orderly development.

A very strong argument can be made, however, against an excessive imbalance in favour of owner-occupiers, as in the case of the factory worker's house. There, inflationary land values increased the value of his assets to the point that, if realized by selling, would amount to a significant misuse of personal property for profit at other's expense. This misuse, moreover, illustrates the unequal opportunities created by heteronomous systems which attempt to equalize the supply of goods and services instead of equalizing local access to basic resources.

[1]For reasons that must be rooted in the peculiarities of local history, the conventional British left condemns private home ownership, failing to make the Marxist distinction between personal and public property which is generally accepted, with regard to homes, in East European countries, as Colin Ward points out in, *Housing: An Anarchist Approach*, Freedom Press, 84B Whitechapel High Street, London E1, 1976

Productivity and resourcefulness

The four cases illustrate two housing systems: the centrally administered or heteronomous system supplying housing to the mason and the government employee, and the locally self-governing autonomous system used by the car painter and the factory worker. The vital differences between these two incompatible systems are to be seen both in their immediate and their longer term effect on the resources they use.

As anticipated in the first two chapters, the bureaucratic heteronomous system produces things of a high standard, at great cost, and of dubious value, while the autonomous system produces things of extremely varied standard, but at low cost, and of high use-value. In the longer run, the productivity of centrally administered systems diminishes as it consumes capital resources, while the productivity of locally self-governing systems increases as it generates capital through the investment of income.

First, consider the most obvious differences between the two housing systems: the housing project residents have little or no choice, they are presented with a package which they must take or leave. The shanty-dweller and the owner-builder, on the other hand, have chosen from several alternatives (which could and should be much wider) and are therefore free to consider the main trade-offs in open housing systems. By having the freedom to live in rent-free shacks, families can keep their options open and maximize their opportunities to gain future security. They are also free to invest in permanent and secure property. Such a family can choose to consolidate its present security at any point, though such a decision would probably close off future options unless property investment in itself opens up future opportunities. These choices involve trade-offs between amenity and assets or between capital outlay and amortization and running costs. The package housing deal presents no such choices once accepted, and the larger the heteronomous package system, the more difficult it becomes to escape the Hobson's choice it imposes.

The other obvious difference is implicit in the names used: locally self-governing systems are diverse by definition. Sponsors, builders, and owners are separate and can combine with the users in an endless variety of ways. Centrally administered systems, on the other hand, bind all the producers and distributors together and also tend to include owners in the same organization, turning all users into tenants of the same landlord or, at least, of the same collective system. The current official endorsements of local participation in modern housing and planning is mainly rhetorical and is self-evidently contrary to the principles of large organizations and centralized administration.

As pointed out in the second chapter, these differences in people's demands on housing would not be relevant if the demands for housing were as standardized as the demands for motor cars. This is a favourite argument of the supporters of mass-production housing who overlook the fact that the complex functions of housing described here cannot be compared to the single and the socially and economically questionable function of cars – transport. Nor would these differences in people's demands be relevant if there was substance to the myth of 'economies of scale' in housing production. But as the evidence of this book demonstrates, big, far from being better, is not only more expensive and more wasteful of resources, but also increases the mis-matches between the provision of, and people's variable demands for housing. And the evidence can be supplemented by studies of all contexts, from the least to the most highly industrialized and institutionalized countries. Only people and local organization – localized housing systems – can provide the necessary variety in housing and the great range of production techniques needed to build it.

The fact that people survive and flourish in such localized

housing systems – as the car painter and the factory worker do – reflects the subtle ineraction between people and their available resources. On the other hand, centralized housing systems can only control relatively scarce and mainly non-renewable resources, so that they are bound to consume disproportionate quantities of capital and to live beyond their means. As Schumacher points out in particularly cogent terms, we have to distinguish between renewable 'primary goods' such as photo-synthetic and metabolic sources of energy, and non-renewable ones such as fossil fuels; and between manufactured products and administered services derived from these two separate sources.[2]

Houses cannot be built or managed and maintained without materials, tools, and the skills to use them, or without land to build on, or without some form of exchange, usually financial credit, with which to obtain resources which the builder does not possess. The financial economy of housing is, of course, a function of the prices of those resources and the costs of the ways in which they are employed. Heteronomous systems are highly dependent on non-renewable resources (and capital), and actually inhibit the generation and use of renewable resources (and income).

Financial resources can be used by both local and central sectors for housing. However, by far the greatest financial resources are the actual and potential savings of the population from their earnings, and these are under their own direct control. This probably represents between 10 and 15 per cent of all personal incomes. It is roughly equivalent to all taxes obtained from incomes and retail sales in an economy such as that of Mexico. (It is proportionately higher in countries with higher per capita incomes, so the same generalization may well hold).[3]

[2] E. F. Schumacher, op. cit. ch.3

[3] Access to the funds governments accumulate for housing expenditure

There are also different *ways* in which resources can be mobilized by central agencies – a question at the heart of the issues raised in the previous chapters. Especially relevant at this point is the alternative of government guarantees for private lending, instead of the public accumulation and direct lending of financial capital. But this illustrates the use of another kind of resource – not finance but legislative powers.

Land is a resource commonly assumed to be controlled by law or corporations, whether public or private. But most land and space for building in Mexico and many other cities is to be found within the existing built-up areas and in small parcels which are commonly regarded as useless by government housing authorities[4]. In Mexico City, especially, there are immense numbers of semi-completed buildings as well as vacant sites within the built-up area that are eventually intended for use. At the same time there are vast and unnecessary new housing projects planned and actually under construction. The big developers, public or private, can only use large areas of land 'efficiently' – so they leap-frog progressively developing areas at enormous

---

and investment is to a great extent dependent on the will of the people to extract it. An increasing number of national governments, including the Federal Government of Mexico, have instituted national systems for compulsory savings from registered employees' wages. It is important to know the relative availability and costs of credits obtained by the factory worker from his employer – and whether the latter would still be available now that employers are obliged to make these institutional contributions.

[4] Dr Alice Coleman of the Department of Geography, King's College, London, has been carrying out a major research on land use in Greater London which shows that there was enough land within the built-up area of 1945 to have accommodated all postwar growth. A case study by Messrs Graham Bennett and Stuart Rutherford, while students at the Architectural Association School of Architecture, London, revealed sufficient land in small unused plots in the London Borough of Newham for at least 4,000 dwellings. This resource was considered 'useless' however by the Borough Council officers as the plots were too small, scattered and irregular to be dealt with by their large and cumbersome administrative machinery.

and unnecessary cost. The steeply sloping site levelled and built up by the factory worker would be deemed unusable by the big developers or, when they do build on such sites, it would be at immense cost.

The other essential material resources may be grouped together under the general heading of *technology*: materials, tools and the skills and labour to use them. That the potential cost savings from owner-built housing is the self-help labour input is a popular misconception. The real technological savings of locally and personally controlled housing systems are from the highly differentiated and therefore flexible, low-energy and generally long-life technologies used such as standardized timber sections and ply-wood and other sheet materials used in the construction of most North American homes (Fig. 37). Of course, by building in ways that minimize the interdependence of different building trades (so one doesn't have to wait for another in order to finish a particular operation) one also maximizes self-help options. These options are used less than is generally supposed, however, as owner-builders rarely contribute more than half the labour input and often hardly any at all. Much the most important self-help savings are made by being one's own general contractor. The other and rarely acknowledged aspect of technology is management. The inefficiency of bureaucratic management is generally recognized and nowhere better than in Parkinson's often quoted law.[5] But self-help management is not only extremely efficient, but also generally represents a far more important money saver than self-help labour.

Of course, for a family or a co-operative group of families, or even a small builder or small local authority to build their own housing, they must have appropriate technologies that allow them to use their own personal resources. Hand tools, small powered tools, easily and cheaply transported materials and locally available skills and labour are the

[5] C. Northcote Parkinson, *Parkinson's Law*, John Murray, London, 1958

common stock-in-trade of local builders. While they can and are all used by large firms as well, the latter tend to use large machines and heavy technologies mainly because they reduce the highly variable human and local inputs which complicate central administration and reduce its productivity. The more traditional local and human technologies are more expensive for a large organization. In other words, central administrations have far less access to loose-fit low-energy and long-life technologies than locally self-governing systems. The usual differences of cost between heteronomous and autonomous housing, when both have equal access to their preferred resources, is naturally and inevitably at least double in the first place and, in the longer run, very many more times than that.

The larger the organization that builds and manages housing, the tighter the fit, the greater the mis-match of housing and households, the lower the effective demand. The higher the energy required and the greater the capital costs, the shorter the lives of the buildings and the greater the costs-in-use.

The issue of housing economy is very simple and straightforward: is it a function of the *productivity* of large organizations or is it a matter of *resourcefulness*, whatever the scale or kind of organization? If it is assumed to be the former, as it is by a vast majority of legislators, administrators, planners and architects – and of course by the big builders – then concern will be concentrated exclusively on improving the efficiency and productivity of the increasingly predominant large-scale industry. But if economy is assumed to be a matter of resourcefulness, or the efficient use of available resources (with particular attention to the differences between capital and income and to the rule of spending less than is earned), then the 'efficiency' of large organizations is evidently counter-productive. In fact, the more they manage to produce, sooner or later, the less there will be to go around. And the time it takes for the chickens to come home to roost depends on the rate at which capital resources are spent.

5. AUTHORITY OVER HOUSING

Personal responsibility versus corporate control

The issue of who really decides what for whom in housing follows from the discussions on housing economies and values raised in the preceding chapters. It has already been shown that the major part of resources invested in housing are those possessed and controlled by the users themselves, and the economies of housing depend on the users' resourcefulness. Resourcefulness and longevity of buildings, as distinct from productivity and short-term costs, require imagination, initiative and above all, personal will to care. As pointed out in chapter three a household's determination to invest their time, efforts, and skills in their homes and surroundings depends on the satisfaction they can expect and the usefulness of their housing. This chapter looks at the issue of authority over housing processes and products, and the problem of demand for housing in the light of the preceding discussions.

The issue of housing value, of usefulness versus material standards, and the issue of housing economy, of local resourcefulness versus centralized productivity, were both illustrated by apparent paradoxes already described. The paradox of the car painter's highly supportive shack and the mason's highly oppressive modern standard house raised the issue of housing value; and the issue of housing economy was raised by the paradox of the factory worker's lower income household, which had substantially larger housing assets than the government employee's higher income household.

Together these present a third paradox: that, in the Mexican context anyway, the demand and will to invest in housing at lower income levels is far greater than that of the substantially higher, moderate income sector. It may even be that the prospects of fulfilling housing demands are generally greater for lower income households, because they are able and willing to build for themselves while moderate income housholds are not, even though they may earn two to three times as much.

This paradox is illustrated by a fifth case history from the field studies by Tomasz Sudra: the case of Mama Elena.

Mama Elena's low-income communal household

Mama Elena, because of her husband's mistreatment, left him to make her living and raise her child independently. Between 1947 and 1962, when Elena moved to her present location, she had moved four times, starting with a servant's room with the middle-class family for which she worked shortly after her arrival. Some years later, Elena became pregnant, lost her job and moved to a *vecindad* (tenement) with her common-law husband. Being an independently-minded person, Elena took up fruit vending while living in the tenement room. The high rent drove the family out to a squatter settlement on the northern periphery. After repeated removals by the police and reoccupations, the family, tired of the insecurity, moved to their present location near a market and a middle-income residential area suitable for her trade and providing job opportunities for her second common-law husband, a lorry driver.

Afraid of repetitions of her earlier experiences of forced removal by police action, the family made no investments and lived in provisional shacks. As there were no apparent moves to eradicate the settlement during the first five years, the family decided to risk investment in permanent building which, they calculated, would consolidate their squatter's claim. Although still fearful of eradication, the household has pursued this policy ever since 1967 and, despite their very low income, Mama Elena and her third (common-law) bricklayer husband have built a 6-room house so far, together with a crude shop on the street (Figs. 26, 27). They share the use of this substantial property with the families of two of Mama Elena's children, and with a third unrelated household which she took under her wing for no apparent material reason.

The 12,000 pesos invested includes contributions from other members of the aggregate household, although the *de facto,* unlegalized property belongs to Elena. She estimated its market value at about 45,000 pesos in 1973 – about five times her own and her husband's combined annual income. If legalized, the property would be worth considerably more than that, but much of the increment would be due to capital gains in the highly speculative free market for building land. The large plot (260 square metres) has enabled a semi-commune of 19 very low income people with unstable incomes to live in relative comfort and security. As a vehicle for the achievement of social and economic security for her approaching old age, Mama Elena's housing strategy has been very sound. (Figs. 22f, 23f).

The adaptability of this user-controlled housing system to varying circumstances is very important. Not long before the interviews, Mama Elena suffered a broken leg which made it impossible for her to continue street vending. So she now continues her trade from a shop built onto the property and this has become a centre of social life from which she dispenses advice to those who come to her for it. The family was thus able to adjust to the major change in their situation after the accident. Neither this adjustment nor the whole procedure which has served the household so well, would have been possible within the rules and regulations governing officially recognized housing procedures and standards.

The full significance of Mama Elena's case is only apparent when it is compared with those of rent-controlled *vecindad* (that is, tenement) dwellers (Figs. 22g,23g), and of subsidized government housing project dwellers (Figs 22c, 23c). Mama Elena's household income, though about twice the subsistence level, was substantially below the metropolitan median income of controlled tenement renters and most government housing project buyers. Unlike Mama Elena, many of the latter have enough cash to pay the key money for a rent-controlled *vecindad*, or to buy a new house in a speculative commercial development, or to pay the bribe usually necessary to obtain a public housing unit. The premiums on such a unit are generally much lower than down-payments for a commercially built house and far less than the key money usually demanded for an inner-city *vecindad*.

As the supply of inner-city tenement accommodation has declined, the prices have naturally risen – in the form of key money where rent controls have been imposed. Key money for a two-room rent-controlled inner city *vecindad* tenement may now be as much as it costs to build a new house twice the size on the periphery. The shrinking and deteriorating *vecindades* are therefore inhabited by a population with a rising income enjoying extremely low rents in highly convenient locations which compensate for the often very poor and overcrowded accommodation.

Mama Elena's household was unambitious and content, economically and socially speaking, to stay where they now live. By contrast, most of the better-off *vecindad* and project households are upwardly mobile, socially and economically, and rapidly so. Their households tended to be nuclear (parents and children only), while Mama Elena's is a multi-nuclear or aggregate household. As such, Mama Elena's household is relatively self-sufficient and the members are mutually supportive. Clearly, they depend far

26

27

Fig. 26. Part of the six-room house built, and being extended, by an aggregate household of three families with 19 members. Although their income is very low, the semi-commune has a relatively stable economy and their security is enhanced by the fact that their (de facto) property is worth four times their joint annual income.

Fig. 27. The adaptability of user-controlled housing to varying circumstances is very important. Unable to continue street vending because of an accident, the female head of the joint household (see Fig. 26), a neighbourhood leader, now runs this small shop built onto the property.

less directly on corporate commercial enterprises and on formal public institutions than the more mobile households of the tenement renters and project buyers who are more frequently dependent on the relatively high wages and salaries of large enterprises and agencies.

Mama Elena's household is dependent, for a sustained income, on the multiciplicity of local enterprises and the fluctuating demands for casual employments by large organizations like construction firms whose demand for labour is especially sensitive to changing public works policies. It is probable that the security provided by the greater number and diversity of local enterprises – and opportunties for self-employment of the kind used by Mama Elena herself – is greater than that provided by the more regular incomes from large organizations which are also subject to political and economic crises.[1]

The tenement renters and project buyers who are locked into the corporate sector – that is, those dependent on large public or private organizations for their incomes – have a very different range of options in housing as well as for jobs and forms of social security. Most people in the corporate sector can choose to build in the local sector – that is, they can squat, or buy land and build outside the controls of the authorities. However, the upwardly mobile moderate income families who do so, usually seek locations and ways that shade into authorized practices, which are acceptable to banking and insurance companies. Since most families in this generally higher income category appear to ignore the non-corporate or informal options, they often have a more limited scope for providing themselves with housing suited to their personal needs.

[1] Lisa Redfield Peattie, author of *The View from the Barrio*, University of Michigan, Ann Arbor, 1968, has been continuing her in-depth studies of the 'informal sector' in Bogota, Colombia. Her preliminary findings show a strong preference among low-income people for the more open-ended jobs and their opportunities than regular wage employment in the formal sector. Advancement in the latter is generally less likely and job-security is often quite uncertain.

Effective, pent-up and potential demands

The cases and situations described here and in previous chapters emphasize the importance of distinguishing the three kinds of housing demand. The differences between what households *can* do and what they *will* do is so great, especially within lower income sectors, that distinctions must be made between effective, pent-up and potential demands, and the non-market demand or, competition, for public housing.

Pent-up demands are those which could be released, or become effective, if households had access to existing options at prices that are in balance with costs and income. Defined in this way, Mama Elena's household has no pent-up demand at all – not only are they satisfied with their condition, but their situation reflects a balanced housing economy. Mama Elena's pent-up demand for housing was released and became an effective demand with her decision to build. Many of the moderate income households renting *vecindades* also have pent-up demands for owner-built 'progressive development' homes like Mama Elena's and that of the factory worker described in the last chapter. The pent-up demands of many *vecindad* households for owner-built homes on the periphery would become effective as soon as they were forced to leave their present dwellings. However, a pent-up demand of this kind can be diverted or perverted into competition for subsidized government housing.

Because public housing is supplied at below market prices, and generally far below cost, the 'demand' for it is of a different order. I have adopted Patrick Crooke's suggestion and call it 'competition' – a competition that is only accessible to categories decided by the administrators of the programmes. Once the 'competition' for the occupancy of subsidized housing has been won, the property may well become the subject of real demands. It is by no means uncommon to find that every unit in well-designed projects in good locations has been sold, rented or sub-let – especially where policing is weak or corruption is strong. This is common whenever the (black-) market price is substantially higher than the value placed on the dwelling by the intended (legal) beneficiaries. When the latter have low incomes or are able to obtain more suitable dwellings for less than the market price, the property is put into circulation, releasing the pent-up demands of higher-income brackets. The adjustments subsequently made are generally beneficial to all concerned. (Though it could be argued, therefore, that it would have been more sensible to give the subsidy in cash in the first place).

To be operationally useful, the concept of potential demand must refer to what people would invest if they had opportunities that matched their priorities. Unlike pent-up demands, potential demands require social and institutional changes and are therefore appropriate only for the setting of long-term goals. If the arguments presented in this book are correct in principle, then centrally administered housing would have to be replaced by a system composed of a multiplicity of locally self-governing sub-systems before this potential demand could be realized.

Needs and priorities

The vital fact that the realization of housing demand depends first on the past experience and future expectations of households, and on their consequent will to invest the resources which only they can control, is generally overlooked. The political reason for this is that the housing shortages generated by the inhibition of local and personal investment, through the inflation of land prices, for instance, work to transfer power to the minorities that control the limited supply of supra-local and centrally controlled resources.

The argument of chapter three, on the values of housing, was that it is what housing *does* for people that matters more than what it *is*, or how it *looks*. And it follows that it is illogical to state housing problems in the modern convention of 'deficits' of units to some material standard. It is just this illogical basis used by centralized housing systems for assessing housing needs that leads to the more or less imaginary demands on which nearly all housing policies are based. To be meaningful and useful as tools for action, people's housing needs must always be stated in terms of *priorities*.

All five cases described in this and the two previous chapters illustrate the variable nature of three universal housing needs – access, shelter, and tenure – each of which must be satisfied within the limits that the household and neighbours concerned can tolerate.

Even to provide a temporary home or abode, a dwelling must give its users *access* to the people, institutions, and amenities on which their livelihoods depend; it must provide a tolerable degree of *shelter* from climate and neighbours; and the users must have a *tenure* long enough to make the move worthwhile. A house can be a home if and only if it is minimally accessible, provides minimum shelter, and a minimum security of tenure. But, as the cases show and as everyone's own experience shows, these limits are immensely variable.

To demonstrate the extent to which these can vary even among people at the same income level, Mama Elena and the car painter had opposite needs: the car painter needed freedom to move at short notice (to take advantage of job opportunities) while Mama Elena's household needed security of tenure even more than proximity to their sources of livelihood to their neighbours, and all these considerably more than a high standard of dwelling construction and amenity.

Another and even more dramatic case among those studied was that of a tubercular middle-aged woman living with her teenage daughter who kept them both alive by working as a prostitute. This would never have happened if the mother, who used to work as a washerwoman for middle-income people in the city, had not been forced to move to the periphery where she exhausted herself trying to work from an inaccessible location. Gross mis-matches of housing priorities and housing obtained can be lethal.

However well-intentioned, the imposition of standardized housing on the false basis of officially presumed 'needs' is potentially murderous. It is ironical that so many personal tragedies are caused by well-meaning professionals and administrators, often with strong ideological motives, who suppose they are contributing to the common people's well-being and even working towards a more just society.

Complexity and control

Even the relatively superficial level of analysis reached in this book shows that the variety of housing demand is immense and therefore requires a highly diversified 'control system' if Ashby's law of Requisite Variety applies. 'If stability is to be obtained, the variety of the controlling system must be at least as great as the system to be controlled'. All the evidence presented suggests that this law does indeed apply to housing. And therefore over-simplified and standardized centralized housing control systems are clearly unstable and can be seen to be breaking down, sometimes literally.

Public housing is more susceptible to financial administrative, and physical breakdown for two reasons. Either because it is more highly centralized, and organized on much larger scales than housing built and managed by private corporations. Or because they are imposed on lower income people who have fewer choices and suffer more directly from mis-matches of the supply and their priorities. This centralization is accentuated by the special constraints of public spending, the administrators of which are obliged to specify both the supply *and* the demand of sectors of the community that cannot afford commercial options in housing. If all public housing agencies were subject to the same financial constraints as private corporations, most would be bankrupt.

Every household, in deciding their own housing priorities, must balance the advantages and disadvantages of each of a complex set of non-monetary, as well as monetary, criteria. To achieve this balance, trade-offs between these various criteria must be made. Realistically, only the household itself can reasonably decide what these trade-offs should be.

On the non-monetary side of the general housing account, there are widely varying priorities for physical amenities and tenancies, which offer significant trade-offs within each area as well as between them. Commonly, trade-offs are made between access to *social* sources of livelihood, usually relatives, and access to *economic* sources, usually workplaces; there are significant trade-offs between the *private* amenities of the dwelling, and the *public* amenities of the immediate surroundings; and there are the very important trade-offs between *security* of tenure, or the option for long-term residence, and *transferability,* or the ease with which an equivalent form of accommodation can be found.

Any particular combination of these alternative priorities must, of course, be economically viable. But, as the analysis of housing economy in the previous chapter explained, the monetary side of the account is also composed of a number of variables and trade-offs: the price paid by the household (for rent or amortization), the market value which may or may not be closely related to its cost, and the assets owned – whether in the form of equity or key money. Clearly these monetary trade-offs are just as important as any of the non-monetary factors and trade-offs listed above.

The rigid hierarchical organization of centrally administered housing policies makes it impossible to satisfy, let alone take advantage of the trade-offs between these complex sets of variable priorities of individual households. Even if these sets of priorities were common to all households, and if there were only a limited number of household situations providing a limited range of alternative demands, a centrally administered system compatible with them all would still be impossibly complex.

Even if it were possible for a centralized decision and control system to supply the great majority of households with well-matched housing services, their tolerance would shrink (thanks to the gift-horse syndrome), generating even more exacting demands while failing to provide that satisfaction which one gets from having made a decision or having done something for oneself, however imperfect it may be.

The complexity and variability of individual household priorities and consequent housing behaviour are beyond the practical grasp of any central institution or organization. If general rules of the kind tentatively indicated in this chapter were developed into proven laws covering the great majority of personal situations in a wide range of contexts, then it would be theoretically possible for a Big Brother central intelligence, with access to sufficient personal data, to programme the provision of suitable housing for all. This obviously undesirable ideal is not only impractical for financial and administrative reasons, but in all probability any successful attempts to 'personalize' institutionally supplied housing would still fail because of the low tolerance for personal goods and services for which the user has no responsibility.

If this is true, then the authority of people over housing in their own localities is critical and, ultimately, it must outweigh all other kinds and levels of authority. Therefore, and probably in all countries and societies in the longer run, householders must be able to make their own critical housing decisions. In the vast majority of cases, only they can know what they need most, and which are the best choice in a given situation.

6. PRINCIPLES FOR HOUSING

The resolution of issues

The last three chapters discussed the basic issues and problems of dwelling environments. The remaining chapters will discuss the principles and practices that follow from the positions taken, and a programme for action.

The three principles to be discussed are suggested by the resolutions of the issues of value in housing, of housing economies, and of authority in housing.

The conclusion – that what matters in housing is what it *does* for people rather than what it *is* – leads to *the principle of self-government in housing*. Only when housing is determined by households and local institutions and the enterprises that they control, can the requisite variety in dwelling environments be achieved. Only then can supply and demand be properly matched and consequently satisfied. And only then will people invest their own relatively plentiful and generally renewable resources.

The next conclusion that the economy of housing is a matter of personal and local resourcefulness rather than centrally controlled, industrial productivity – leads to *the principle of appropriate technologies for housing*. Only if the mechanical and managerial tools available are used by people and small organizations can locally accessible resources be effectively used.

The third conclusion that people in their own localities have ultimate authority over housing, as investment and care depend on resources that only they can use economically, leads to *the principle of planning for housing through limits*. Only if there are centrally guaranteed limits to private action can equitable access to resources be maintained and exploitation avoided. As long as planning is confused with design and lays down lines that people and organizations must follow, enterprise will be inhibited, resources will be lost, and only the rich will benefit.

Elements of action

Practical activity and effective action is what we and existence are all about. As well as being stimulated by them, actions lead to problems. And problems raise issues. Issues, in turn, indicate principles for action, while principles determine the resolution of issues. And finally, principles are guides for practice as well as being generated by it. These elements in the development of a process for action must be fully recognized for any coherent discussion of social, institutional and environmental change. The Geddesian square provides the conceptual frame of reference: (Fig. 28)[1]. It is symptomatic of pseudo-science

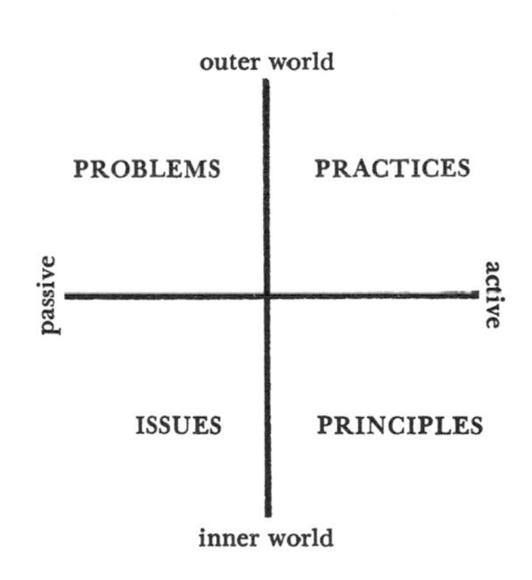

Fig. 28. *Four Elements of Action*. Following Patrick Geddes' interpretation of the classic and universal differentiation of inner and outer realities, and of active and passive modes of being, essential differences and complementarities of the elements of action are clarified. The most common confusions today are between general issues and particular problems, and between general principles and particular practices. When treated synonymously, issues and problems lead to useless generalizations or blindness to others' experience. When principle is confused with practice, action is locked into rigid programmes or it becomes incoherently empirical.

[1] Paffard Keating Clay and John F. C. Turner, *The Geddes Diagrams: Their Contribution Towards a Synthetic Form of Thought*, in: *Patrick Geddes*, 2nd ed. 1949, op. cit. Ch. 2

that issues and principles are either denied or confused with problems and practices.

Failure to understand and act on the essential differences between issues and problems, and between principles and practices exacerbate the three common abuses diagnosed in this chapter.

The principle of self-government in housing

First, there is the failure to separate personal and local activities and their immediate ends from those that are necessarily standardized at supra-local levels. Examples of these two extremes are houses and cars. People's homes are unique by definition – although a house is a relatively simple assembly, it has an immensely complex and variable set of uses. Motor cars, on the other hand, are relatively complex machines but they are necessarily designed for very simple uses – transportation. It is proving as disastrous to build and manage houses in ways that impose standardized housing types and life-styles, as it would be to fail to impose rules for driving powerful (and necessarily standardized) machines at high speeds in public places.

The principle of appropriate technologies of housing

The second failure discussed in this chapter is the confusion between centrally administered systems and self-governing ones, and the consequences of the domination of the former as the preferred modern means for achieving all immediate ends. Corporate organizations and the generally heavy and centralizing technologies they use have totally different capabilities from local and autonomous organizations, which generally use light and decentralizing technologies. While there may be arguments in favour of the small-scale production of high quality motor cars, it seems unlikely that this could compete with the mass-production that so successfully replaced it. The mass production of housing, on the other hand, is intrinsically uneconomic as well as socially and ecologically destructive for the reasons given in the previous chapters.

The principle of planning for housing through limits

The third failure discussed is the confusion of essentially different ways of controlling organized activity. Actions may be controlled by obliging the actors to follow lines for procedures, or they may be controlled by setting the limits to what the actors may do on their own initiative and in their own ways. To continue with the example of homes and cars, it is obvious that car manufacturing should be highly standardized, and that car drivers must be obliged not only to keep to the roads, but also to the same side! Home-builders, managers, and users, on the other hand, will be unable to invest all their resources or get the full use-values from the end products unless they are free to use the resources available to them, in their own ways – that do not limit the freedom of others or harm future generations.

Packages and Parts

Consider the extremes between heteronomy and autonomy in air travel. Everyone experiences heteronomy whether they are aware of it or not. The user is clearly 'subject to the rule of another being or power', and most passengers are only too glad to be in the hands of a competent and authoritarian air crew.

Autonomy is equally obvious in its more extreme forms. Pedestrians have complete control over their legs and can virtually go where they please. Most instances, however, fall between these two extremes, as most decisions and controls governing particular activities are composites of heteronomy and autonomy. For instance, the motor car – where, although drivers are bound by certain heteronomously administered restraints (roads and traffic regulations) they exercise their autonomy in choosing where they wish to go, and by what route.

These same extremes, and shades between, exist in housing – as the case histories show. Modern public housing tenants have little control over where they live or what kinds of dwellings and local amenities they have, and no control at all over the design and construction of their homes, or even over the ways in which they are managed and maintained. Not only Robinson Crusoe but most peasants (all castaways in their own ways) decide and do all of these things for themselves, within the often narrow limits of what they can and are free to do, of course. Their autonomy is limited only by their control over resources.

One vital difference between autonomy and heteronomy in housing services is that network (autonomous) organizations make loose parts available, while hierarchic (heteronomous) systems supply packages.

Simon Nicholson's Theory of Loose Parts[2] reminds us that freedom to do things for ourselves and in our own ways depends on the availability of a limited number of components that can be assembled in a maximum number of different ways. One must also remember that the returns on an increasing number of parts diminishes very rapidly. In most cases we need only a very few with which to do an immense range of variations. For example, consider the number of words, syntaxes and languages that can be written with a couple of dozen letters. Communication would be reduced, not increased, by a larger alphabet, since it would make reading more difficult to learn and thus reduce literacy.

Packaging is the most effective way of depriving people of control over their own lives and of alienating the products. Packaging, or the heteronomous packagers, achieve this in

[2] Simon Nicholson, *The Theorgy of Loose Parts*, reprinted in *Landscape Architecture*, USA, October 1971; reprinted in *Bulletin on Environmental Education*, Town & Country Planning Association, London, April, 1972

two ways: by maximum processing they complicate the product and supply it in mysterious and opaque forms, often enclosed in shiny shells and booby-trapped. If they are not actually dangerous to tamper with, many typical modern products are virtually useless as soon as they go wrong; they are so expensive to repair that it is cheaper to throw them away and get another – to the great profit of the manufacturers and suppliers. Packaged foods are not very different: not only is one paying a high price for the containers, which often represent higher energy inputs than the energy outputs of their contents, but more and more processed foods are prepared for unique uses. Try using a cake mix for a different kind of cake!

Packaged housing is notoriously inflexible; it burns up a great deal more energy, and generally has a much shorter life than housing assembled by small builders from combinations of local and imported materials and components in response to local demands.

These large-scale housing projects are burdened with a large administrative organization employing many professionals and highly paid administrators, as well as disproportionately large numbers of often very poorly paid but also non-productive white-collar workers. At the other extreme, customary and almost entirely self-governing squatter settlements, or the intermediate situation of the legal owner-builder or co-operative association, carry hardly any direct overheads at all.

While such extremes are more apparent in these lower income countries, the unbearable expense of centrally administered, package-housing services is also excessive in upper income countries.

The cost of packaged housing

For people, the value of housing lies in what it does for them. It is not so much a function of what it looks like and what it is for the architects and builders, bankers and speculators and short-term politicians. Their view of rigid packaging of standardized housing types, management systems and residential areas prevents them from seeing use-values. The use-values of these large housing projects in all parts of the world are very low. So low, in fact, that most households' energies are concentrated on getting out instead of caring. Carelessness and vandalism are the hallmarks of modern mass housing.

The often well-intentioned policies based on mass housing are very costly ways of impoverishing people – first the poor and, in the longer run, society as a whole. In low and very low income economies, it is especially obvious that the demand for labour does not serve those who have the greatest needs, but those who have the greatest surplus. The greater people's margin of savings the greater their expenditure on products such as colour television sets which are not only of dubious existential value, but also provide far fewer opportunities for responsible and creative work, both for producers and for users.

The argument that the rich generate development by employing the poor does not bear close examination. Nor do the arguments that the rich feed the poor from the crumbs of their tables, or that they clothe and house them in their filtered-down cast-offs. The poor will only eat, clothe, and house themselves better if they are more fully employed and better paid. And this depends, as the analysis presented in this book has demonstrated, on the implementation of the three principles described in this chapter – the third of which demands the differentiation and proper application of *executive* and *legislative* planning, which are the alternative ways of employing organizations for specific ends.

Executive or legislative planning

The differences between kinds of organization are critical. Their influence on planning can reinforce one against another in any particular sphere. The type of organization is clearly a major determinant of resources used, production systems, and the values of the goods and services produced.

Choosing the correct type of organization is the major planning problem, drawing the boundaries between the spheres of action by centrally admininstered and locally self-governing systems. More precisely, it is the problem of limiting the mix between these two systems so that one does not cripple the other.

The predominant way in which planning is carried out is what I call *executive* planning. This is planning by programmed specifications and procedures. This is often called 'urban design' and is deeply embedded in contemporary planning theory and practise.[3]

Unlike the sponsors of modern mass housing projects and their 'urban designers', King Edward II of England 'ordered' his new towns, as he put it, *before* the 'arrayment' of the urban 'accoutrements'. In more modern words, the planners got the people together before the town was built, and the latter were given a great deal more freedom to decide for themselves what to build. King Phillip II of Spain's highly successful town planning 'Law of the Indies' which regulated many colonial cities in the sixteenth and seventeenth centuries, was essentially similar. Both were much nearer to the planning and development procedures of the squatter settlement than to the housing project. As the principal purpose of the new towns was to earn revenue – in other words, to generate development – the kings minimized rather than maximized initial investment and concentrated on ensuring the maximum investment by

[3] In a letter quoted by N. Evenson in *Chandigarh*, University of California Press, Berkeley, California, 1966, an eminent architect wrote: 'Le Corbusier, Jeanneret and I are all architects heavily involved in town planning. Any architects worth their name in charge of building on these scales of this city must have strong ideas on planning as being undisputedly an extension of architecture.'

their subjects. This was done, and often with considerable success, simply by setting out the *limits* of what they were free to do. This took the form of demarcated plots and guarantees of secure tenure. In return, the beneficiaries were obliged to invest to a minimum level within a given period, or forfeit their tenure.

This latter and more traditonal kind of organization, where planning sets limits within which people and their enterprises may do as they will, I call *legislative* planning. The laws employed here are *pro*-scriptive rather than *pre*-scriptive – that is, they are norms and institutions that set limits to what people and local enterprises *may* do, rather lines which they *must* follow. Of course, there is no clear threshold between limits and lines – as limits get closer together they become lines – and some lines may be so faint that the follower has to find his own way.

This statement of the central problem of planning – of first differentiating between executive lines of action and legislative limits to action, and then drawing up those lines and, much more importantly, those limits – is a reminder of our own ignorance. One cannot place limits on some activity without understanding it. This uncomfortable truth is illustrated by the fact that the only area where substantial progress has been made towards limits for housing and building action is in construction. We know enough about the functional characteristics of materials to have performance standards for the design of *construction.* Performance standards set limits, as distinct from the old-fashioned specification standards which lay down the lines. Every architect appreciates the difference between being obliged by law to build load-bearing walls for houses to an 11-inch cavity wall specification, and being free to build a wall in any way he and his client please, as long as they can prove that it will carry the loads placed on it and provide the necessary degrees of insulation.

But we do not know enough, or we have not organized

our knowledge well enough, to do the equivalent for the design of *space,* or for the design of its *management,* or for the design of building *economy.* This is natural enough given the immense disparity of knowledge between the natural sciences, as they used to be called, and the human sciences. In other words, without a theory of the built environment, we cannot write its laws. And if we cannot write its laws, we can only design and build in an *ad hoc* way – we cannot really plan at all.

This may be an exaggeration and if we rearranged the knowledge we already have, we could probably formulate practical performance standards for environmental design that would generate social and economic as well as physical

Fig. 29. A squatter's permanent house under construction in Arequipa, Peru. The provisional thatched hut is inside the stone walls and will be dismantled when the concrete roof slab is built. This will provide the floor for the next storey, as in the case of the house in the upper left-hand corner of the photograph.

29

harmony. To take one example which has excellent historical as well as contemporary precedents: the rule that both minimum *and* maximum construction standards must be proportionate to their life span. I am sure that neither King Edward II nor King Phillip II prohibited the construction of provisional shacks by their subjects while the latter were preparing to build their permanent homes. Sir Thomas More's description of house-building in *Utopia* certainly reflects sixteenth century procedures and it is an excellent description of what most squatter-builders aspire to, and a surprising number actually achieve:

> Houses in the beginning were very low, and like homely cottages or poor shepherd houses, made at all adventures of every rude piece of timber that came first to hand, with mud walls, and ridged roofs, thatched over with straw. But now the houses be curiously builded after a gorgeous and gallant sort, with three stories one over another. (Fig. 29).

It goes without saying that few contemporary planning authorities would tolerate such untidy methods, in spite of the immense economies and social advantages[4]. They prohibit progressive development which is dependent on the will of autonomously organized people and communities. And that is in conflict with the heteronomous control institutions maintain over them.

[4] As this was going to press, Mr. Bakri Abdelrahim described an exceptional programme to his fellow participants in the Special Programme on Housing in Urban Development (which I direct at the Development Planning Unit, University College of London). 12,000 households, half the population of Port Sudan (on the Red Sea), have been settled on planned plots in less than four years and at minimal cost. By tying the length and conditions of leases to levels of investment, all income levels participate and up-grading is maximized. Planning permissions for changes of use, for shops and workshops, for instance, are automatic when agreed by neighbours. Neighbourhoods decide for themselves how their share of the limited budget for improvements are to be used. By the criteria of this essay this is the most successful example of planned urban development I know of – and it practises the principles identified above.

7. THE PRACTICE OF HOUSING BY PEOPLE

The Solution of problems

This chapter discusses how the principles identified may be put into practice. It deals with the issues and problems of the alternative ways, means and ends in housing which are the subject of this book.

The three practical problems of housing policy are discussed here: planning effective strategies (the ways); identifying practical policy instruments (the means); and setting realistic policy goals (the ends). The implementation of these three aspects of housing action is analogous to the organization of a professional football club. The club directors must devise the best *ways* to use the club's resources, planning effective strategies. Their *means,* their policy instruments, are the players, coaches and trainers as well as their fields and funds. The *end* is to score as many goals as possible.[1]

As any follower of Football understands, the role of the club's directors is not to score goals. And it is just as foolish for central government to attempt to provide houses. Effective government housing strategies are those centrally administered policies that protect and make available scarce resources.

When a club has only limited funds it is courting disaster if it chooses to import a costly professional. He will be expensive to maintain and contribute little to improve the play of the rest of the team. More sensibly, the club will use its resources to provide facilities for their own local players.

[1]I am indebted to Haig Beck for this analogue.

In the same way, countries with limited resources do little to improve their over-all housing problems by embarking on isolated programmes to construct modern standard housing schemes. Instead, such countries (and this term 'limited resources' is relative as it includes all countries) are better at improving the service infrastructure that will enable and stimulate the local provision of housing.

It is not the purpose of a local football club to provide mass entertainment. The real end of football is recreation – of which spectating is only an aspect. And the best use-value of the sport is when it is played at a local level where both players and spectators have equal opportunities to participate – if not on the field, then as part of the team's back-up. The analogy can be extended to the use-values of housing: The real use-value of housing cannot be measured in terms of how well it conforms to the image of a consumer society standard. Rather, it must be measured in terms of how well the housing serves the household. As the case studies of this essay have demonstrated, appearance has little to do with use, and the individual's direct participation in providing his own housing not only ensures more useful homes, but tends in time to create better housing than the big league ideal.

Planning effective strategies

Economy and resourcefulness highlight the relativity of authority in housing. While central organizations have indisputable powers to use certain kinds of tools and resources, such as industrial mass production, they may have little or none over others, such as personal care of dwellings built. A necessary first step, therefore, is to recognize the matching of levels of action and authority which establishes the institutional framework within which any policy must be considered.

Housing, or any specific dwelling environment, is an assembly of components, and no component can be built or provided without tools, materials and skill (i.e. technology), and exchange, usually finance. By this definition, there are three levels of action, each of which demand different scales and kinds of organization and different mixes of skill, and each level of action therefore offers quite different opportunities for participation. These levels of action are local, municipal, and central government.

At the local level, opportunities most commonly considered and practised centre on the design, construction, and management of dwellings and their immediate surroundings – that is, on the assembly of sub-divided land, infrastructure and services and buildings. This complex process demands many skills, from the ability to negotiate land purchases and property transfers to plastering ceilings. The case studies in this book have demonstrated that when the processes of housing-assembly take place on a small scale they not only offer economies, but are also likely to satisfy the highly variable priorities of users.

It is nevertheless clear that while the assembly of dwelling environments can and traditionally does take place at local levels and on a small scale, most types of infrastructure and many public services demand action at larger scales. Most water supply systems, for instance, are of district or metropolitan scale, and public transport is often organized on still larger scales without apparent diseconomies.

The planning and management of basic resources is generally carried out on the largest scales – regional, national or even international. While it can be argued that with the production of cement, for example, in countries with low per capita incomes and inadequate transportation systems, the distribution and pricing is almost certain to be tied into national or international markets. Land, anyway, must be subject to governmental controls if it is not to be exploited by private interests. And, as long as housing depends on long-term credit to a significant extent, housing finance is bound to be a major concern of national government policy.

Systems for the production or generation and supply of technological resources, land and finance are relatively simple as well as being subject to central controls and large-scale organization. However, this is not to say these elements should or even can be directly produced and supplied by central agencies. What is being suggested is that central agencies are limited to the necessarily large-scale operation of controls determining local *access* to resources. The above is not an argument in support of land nationalization, that is, the centralized acquisition and distribution of land – which may even reduce the availability of land for local users. Rather, it is an argument in support of legislative controls *limiting* the concentration of resources (that is, wealth) and, therefore, of power, and their misuse. In the case of land, this principle suggests community trusteeship within national law, rather than nationalization in the sense of direct public ownership as an alternative to the commercialization of land.[2]

The above suggests a 'normal' correlation between levels of action and scales of organization and authority – another way of describing the relationships analyzed in chapter one above and in Figures 8 and 9 – that may be set out as follows (Fig. 30).

The appropriate patterns of authority and action suggested here are in sharp contrast to those in the modern or would-be industrialized world. In countries where production and distribution are dominated by more or less independent capitalist corporations, and where land is owned privately and commonly valued as a speculative investment rather than for its usefulness, the general pattern of housing authority and action is almost reversed (Fig. 31).

[2] Robert E. Swann, *The Community Land Trust, A Guide to a New Model of Land Tenure in America,* International Independence Institute, Ashby, Mass. USA.

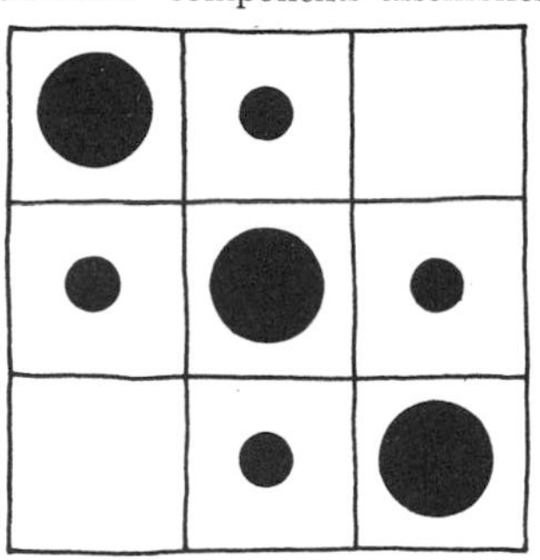

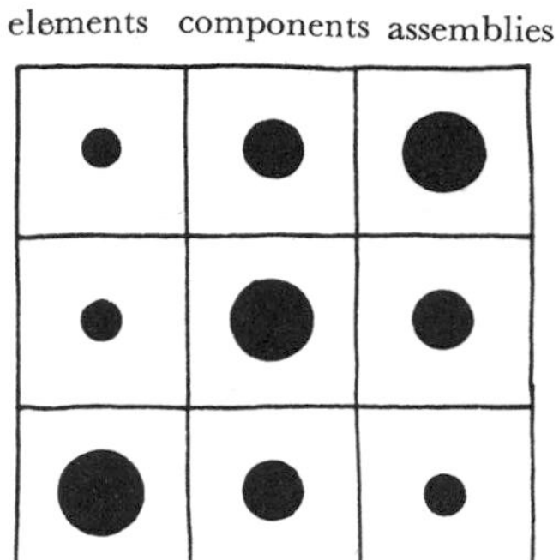

Fig. 30. A normal distribution of levels of action and authority in which central governments' role is to guarantee equal access to basic resources, in which municipal government's role is to provide infrastructure, and where local communities and enterprises build and maintain dwelling environments.

Fig. 31. A common distribution of levels of action and authority in which central government's dominant role is the provision of dwelling environments, and in which land and finance are controlled mainly by the private sector.

This operational distinction between centrally administered programmes which substitute for activities that are traditionally controlled locally, and the provision of supports enabling local action, is critical. Understood in these social and institutional terms, Habraken's concept of supports for housing points directly to what must be done.[3] His perhaps unintended analogue developed in technological terms emphasizes the necessity of differentiating between those elements in housing demanding greater stability and those that lend themselves to flexibility. And it coincides precisely with the principles identified above.

Once these distinctions have been grasped, it is perfectly clear that housing forms cannot be viably programmed by central agencies. Modern administrations, from the World Bank to the smallest and poorest national agencies, are trapped in the syndrome symptomized by categorical

[3] John Habraken, *Supports*, Architectural Press, London 1972. (First published in Holland in 1961)

programmes. As long as thought, planning and institutions demand the classification of demand and supply and their combination in fixed categories around which goals, instruments and strategies are organized, no real or direct progress will be made towards the liberation of resources, the realization of their potential and the regeneration of culture.

The necessity of reducing the scale of authority as the complexity of action increases, is a function of Ashby's principle of requisite variety. Dwelling environments are necessarily functions of their inhabitants and, as people's housing priorities are extremely varied (as the evidence presented in this book suggests), control of dwellings and neighbourhoods must be in personal and local hands. Conversely, where larger scale is required, there will be a greater degree of standardization in the infrastructure – as in the resource supply systems on which particular environments depend – and there will be a greater need for central planning and even administration, of these subsystems or submarkets.

This proposition is supported by massive evidence that social and material returns on centrally administered investments are inversely proportional to the scale and complexity of the operations demanded.

Experience shows that more public monies are lost than recovered, and very rarely are there any positive returns when investments are made in 'low-cost' housing projects for low income people. This is normal and acceptable when the beneficiaries are satisfied and, of course, when subsidies are generally available. But this is not acceptable in the more usual situations where further investment depends on the recovery of those already made. Experience with the installation of public utilities and the provision of public services, the components of which can accept a far greater degree of standardization, on the other hand, show much smaller direct losses and can often be shown to have provided substantial indirect returns through widening the tax base. The fact that many utility companies are privately owned and operated, even in low income areas, shows that they can be profitable. The greatest returns of all, however, are achieved when public investments are made for the provision of scarce basic resources.

The example of the highly productive mortgage-guarantee programme of the United States is often held up as one of the most successful housing policies ever carried out. The productivity of that programme during the decades following the Second World War is undeniably immense in proportion to the public cost. That it could have been greater still, had there been a matching programme of land-price controls, and that it could have avoided the further polarization of ethnic and class groups, had bankers provided mortgages to owner-builders as readily as to commercial developers, only emphasizes the vital importance of a socially orientated, national resources planning system. The success of this United States case, along with some Latin American programmes for appropriately administering resources, clearly shows the importance of distinguishing between the limitations of categorical programmes and the advantages of open support systems.[4]

An effective strategy for housing depends on the

[4] Observations that I made in my working paper, *Uncontrolled Urban Settlements: Problems and Policies* (for the United Nations International seminar on Urbanization Problems and Policies at the University of Pittsburgh in 1966) stimulated interest in the current change-over from conventional housing schemes to sites and services programmes. I fear that they may prove to be more effective instruments in the hands of oppressive governments, unless, as I still hope, the consequently increased focus on the social use of finance, land and infrastructure leads out of the categorical programme syndrome – the assumption that the problem is to provide categories of people with classified bundles of housing goods and services. A small but clear illustration of the alternative is given in one of my contributions in *Freedom to Build*, op. cit., *The Re-education of a Professional*, pp 139-144

practicality of the patterns of authority operating at all levels of housing action. The overall strategy suggested by the above interpretation is to *reverse* the most common priorities for government investment in housing. At present, especially in lower income and rapidly urbanizing countries with the most acute problems, governments commonly invest more in projects for housing lower income people than in infrastructure – and rarely is any attention paid to the distribution or generation of basic resources such as land and money for local non-commercial investment.

Only in this way can more and better housing be achieved wihout either robbing other productive sectors of the economy or the poorer sectors of the community. Only if the major and under- or misused personal and local resources are released by the proper matching of levels of action and authority can housing improvement occur at all in low income countries, or be maintained in countries of high incomes or per capita budgets.

Practical Policy Instruments

The two kinds of instruments needed for any operation are, of course, technological and managerial – whether the 'tools' are football club players or building techniques. There are, however, significant degrees of variation within each of these interdependent elements. While there is evidently a tendency for organizations and tehcnologies to match each other in scale, power, and weight, it is not necessarily true that the larger the management the more energy-intensive the tools they use. Very large and highly centralized, hierarchic organizations have existed from early historical times: the Pharoahs matched an extremely simple technology with a very sophisticated and complex managerial organization.

The corollary does not hold, however, because more sophisticated and complex machines demand back-up organizations that are directly proportional to their power and weight. As the Pharoahs demonstrated, very large organizations can use man-powered hand tools. Machine-powered hand tools which can take most of the drudgery out of work, do not demand very large or complex organizations for their manufacture, distribution or servicing, but complex heavy machinery does.

As long as local makers and suppliers agree to standardize components, there can be very large numbers of small power-tool makers. This is less true for bulldozers, for instance, and not at all true for huge cement manufacturing plants currently held to be the most 'economic'. Centralized management tends to use the most powerful machines at its disposal. Karl Marx would undoubtedly have modified his remarkable statement that, 'if you have too many useful machines you get too many useless people' if he had foreseen the potential of modern lightweight and (potentially) decentralizing technologies. Today he might say that if you have too many useful but powerful machines you get too many powerless as well as useless people.

The issues of management and technology are functions of economy. Underlying this is the issue of resourcefulness versus industrial productivity. The use of non-renewable resources must be minimized, and most renewable resources for housing are in personal and local hands. This being so, managerial and technological appropriateness will be judged by the ease with which they can be handled by local citizens and small organizations. The truly economic scale of building and maintaining the dwelling environment is small. The tautological phrase 'economies of scale' merely means that any particular system has an optimum scale of operation. That it is commonly assumed to mean 'bigger is better' is part of the urban-industrial syndrome.

Along with the level of energy demanded, the combination of technology and management determines both fitness and life or durability. Economy of energy, adaptability, and longevity in housing all depend on small-scale assembly and local control.

These observations are anticipated by Simon Nicholson's 'Theory of Loose Parts' which, in a modified form that recognizes the law of diminishing returns may be stated as follows:

In any environment both the degree of inventiveness and creativity, and the possibility of discovery are directly proportional to the number of ways in which the required number of variables can be combined.
This rule recognises Ockham's Razor and complements Ashby's principle of requisite variety.

Mass-produced building parts may often have longer potential lives than their hand-made equivalents. Take modern plywoods for example. There can be little doubt that this same sheet material which has a potentially indefinite life, is far more likely to deteriorate along with the buildings of which it forms a part when used in a centrally administered housing project than when used in an owner-built or owner-occupied home. From the growing mass of evidence it can also be argued that potentially long-life building materials and components will last less in mass-produced assemblies. This is particularly so when they are locked together in industrially produced building systems. The strongest element is just as good as the whole assembly's weakest link.

It is most important, however, to understand the theory of loose parts in administrative as well as in technological terms. The rigidity with which categories of households are linked with types of financing, for intance, can do as much damage to the economy of housing as the imposition of construction systems demanding patented components.

In Britain, first-time mortgage loans are generally only available to young married couples and then for new or newer standard houses. The mis-matches inherent in this rigid system of housing finance can be intolerable for potential home-owners. Few young married couples can afford to buy new homes and few can obtain finance for the cheaper substandard houses they could improve in time from their own renewable resources. Many young couples are consequently forced to accept publicly financed rented accommodation which is heavily subsidized or to rent substandard accommodation which they have no incentive to maintain or improve. Lower income older married couples are generally excluded from the first-time mortgage market, as are single lower income people and unmarried couples.

This indissoluble marriage of mortgage loans to new or newer standard houses available only to buyers with little or no collateral greatly reduces the effective demand for private sector housing, at least in urban-industrial societies, as well as greatly reducing the supply of improved lower-cost older dwellings.

In general, modern systems must be dis-aggregated, not destroyed. To suppose that the principles of loose fit, low energy and small scale exclude modern management, science and technology is as absurd as to suppose that long life can only be achieved with pre-industrial tools and techniques. What is being argued is that large organizations should have little or no business building or managing dwelling environments. Instead, they should be doing a great deal more busines installing infrastructure and manufacturing and supplying tools and materials that people and their own small enterprises can use locally. There is plenty of room for debate over the extent to which central administrations are in fact necessary for specific components of infrastructure – such as the generation and distribution of electric power, or the manufacture of cement. There are many who hold that electricity should be generated and cement manufactured by large numbers of smaller plants.[5] As in these and most other cases, any general rules are modified by regional and local circumstances. There is much less room for debating the necessity of separating subsystems wherever their potential for variability is inhibited by their loss of identity in a larger system – however dependent they may be on it. And the same principle applies to players in a football team as to component subsystems in a house.

Setting Realistic Policy Goals

The underlying issues of the meaning and value of housing were discussed in Chapter 3. It revealed that, in practice, conventional policy goals for increasing centrally administered mass-production of new houses enriches the better off, the commonly very rich sponsors, senior functionaries and professionals, at the expense of the most needy in low-income contexts. The evidence also suggests that categorical programmes and housing schemes destroy local communities, and their own potential for providing economic solutions to their own real problems.

In order to be realistic and constructive, policy goals must be restated in terms that describe the proper matching of people and their environments and of their own contributions with the value of the services they get. The problem of translating these principles into practical rules can be solved only through the formulation of performance standards.

Performance standards set limits to what practitioners *may* do. In contrast, conventional 'specification' standards lay down lines which practitioners *must* follow. The vital distinction between *pro*-scriptive or limit-setting law, and

[5] The general issues are raised and discussed in G. Foley, *The Energy Question*, Penguin Books, London, 1976. The specific case of cement manufacture is analyzed in a working paper by the Intermediate Technology Development Group, Parnell House, Wilton Road, London SW1

pre-scriptive or line-laying regulations was pointed out in the last chapter. We cannot plan legislatively – that is through proscriptive law or limits that guarantee freedom of action without exploitation. This *ad hoc* approach has led inevitably to confusing environmental planning with architectural design – a consequence that architects are tempted to welcome and which has reinforced the megalomania of those that have succumbed to 'success'.

The historical precedents referred to in the last chapter suggest that we may not be as ignorant as it might suit some sectors to maintain. The proscriptive limits to action planning techniques used by Edward II of England and Phillip II of Spain met with genuine success. While it is true that they had much simpler technologies and administrations to contend with, their successes point in directions that could lead to an up-dating of principles that were lost in the flood of urban-industrial speculative development and that were overlooked by the nineteenth and twentieth century reformers. With few exceptions, these have sided either with commercial interests determined to use land and credit for private profit, or with those for whom the only alternative is centralized socialization or 'nationalization'. Only now is the more traditional alternative of localized trusteeship reasserting itself. This is an up-to-date version of systems common throughout the pre-industrial world in which only the *use* of land can be owned. Rights to such an assignment of usufruct are invested in the local community.

The recent and growing interest in the so-called 'informal' sector – whether in housing and urban settlement or in small industry and local commerce – also indicates another possible area of proscriptive legislative action. Such legislation is necessary to protect the access these local sector groups require to resources. However, to be truly effective, the legislators would have to enter the 'no-go' areas of economic self-interest and industrial relations.

The failures of well-meant but misguided attempts by legislators to provide for housing action in the form of centrally administered sites and services programmes will provide valuable experiences and should lead to corrections at least, in contexts not dominated by capitalism in its private or public forms. The restatement of problems and the redirection of policy goals are perhaps the hardest as well as the first and pre-requisite steps in the restructuring of housing – or built environment – policy. But many planners, architects and urban development administrators are already turning round to face the fact that their real authority has quite different limits to those we have been brought up to suppose. If it is indeed true that human society depends on personal responsibility for the full and proper use of its resources, then the more activities that are centrally prescribed, the less will be done and the greater the costs. The poorer we are or become, the greater the urgency for proscriptive rules that support and stimulate the generation of self-ordering form.

8. PARTICIPATION IN HOUSING

Whose participation in whose decisions?

The current debate on citizen participation and local development takes very different forms in rich and poor countries. This chapter discusses the issue in language more commonly used in high-income contexts while using illustrations from low-income contexts. This is intended not only to highlight the universality of the issues, principles and practices involved, but also to show how much can be learned by the rich from the poor.

In countries where the great majority are poor, 'citizen participation' is not seen as an exceptionally advanced form of democracy. The fact that the great majority in pre-industrial and rapidly urbanizing countries build their own homes and settlements is seen in different ways. Not long ago this was universally regarded as an undesirable characteristic of 'under-development' and institutional and technological 'backwardness'. Now the most informed and serious debate is between those who see the necessity for local housing action as a symptom of internal and external 'dependencies' – the current euphemism for exploitation of the poor by the rich – and those, like myself, who go beyond this rather obvious fact to see the immense potential it represents. The current practices of literal self-help home-building by under-nourished and over-worked people without credit, with inadequate tools and poor materials is not presented here as a model. Many have accused Mangin, myself and others[1] of romanticizing the truly hard

[1] William P. Mangin, ed., *Peasants in Cities,* Houghton Mifflin, Boston, 1969

conditions of ordinary people in most world cities because they have failed to differentiate between the practices we describe and the principles we perceive – perhaps because we have not spelled the latter out with sufficient clarity. Even readers of *Freedom to Build* tend to assume that my co-authors and I are writing about 'self-help' in the narrow and literal sense of do-it-yourself building and so relegate the basic principles of 'dweller control' to a special corner or sector of the housing system. This book, and this chapter in particular, is another attempt to correct this misunderstanding and pepper the trail laid by the red herring of self-help. As pointed out in *Freedom to Build,* the obligation to build your own house could be as oppressive as being forbidden to do so – the corollary of the freedom to literally build your own house is the freedom *not* to have to. If significant material or human benefits can be obtained from self-help construction, which are obvious enough from the precedents in all contexts, those who wish to take advantage of them will be deprived, very seriously in many cases if they are not free to do so.[2] It is clear from the preceding chapters, however, that this is a relatively secondary issue. The central issue is that of *control* or of the powers to *decide:* Who actually does what follows from and is therefore secondary to the initial directives. This is what citizen participation is really all about: whose participation in whose decisions?

The Desirability of Participation

The economic desirability of local citizen's participation in housing (design, construction and management – i.e. at the level of assembly) depends on two open questions: (1) the relative efficacy of centrally administered systems of housing provision and (2) the effects of local participation on the productivity of such systems.

[2] William Grindley, *Owner-builders: Survivors with a Future,* in *Freedom to Build*, op. cit. Ch. 1

These modern housing supply systems contrast sharply with traditional systems which are networks of independent local builders and suppliers generally contracted by small proprietors and individual households. In its most developed form users of local networks have access to modern credit facilties as well as fully serviced building land and modern construction materials and equipment (as in most small town and suburban areas of the United States).[3] The less developed systems by which most dwellings and localities in low income countries are built are essentially the same. Network forms of organization are locally self-governing as works are carried out by any variety of locally available contractors in response to the decisions and orders of local investors (whether these are individuals or proprietors, voluntary housing bodies[4], cooperatives, or local community government).

Positions on the issue of centrally administered versus locally self-governing systems of housing provision vary between the extremes at which protagonists deny the viability of the other, to intermediate or oscillating positions dependent on particular cases or contexts. Those that assume a higher potential for centralized housing systems, with or without the industrialization of building construction, generally regard the more localized and traditional procedures as intrinsically less desirable. It is often assumed that small-scale local development, construction and management procedures for housing are bound to produce inferior goods and services. At the other extreme, there are those who have concluded that large organizations, especially if they employ industrialized

[3] William Grindley, op. cit. Ch. 1

[4] 'Voluntary housing bodies' refers to private, non-profit and charitable organizations such as the Peabody Trust (set up by a philanthropist from Massachusetts which built many improved tenements in London late in the last century) and housing societies and associations (such as those now being supported by the British government through the semi-public Housing Corporation as an alternative to municipal housing).

buildings systems, have a substantially lower economic potential and are bound to produce socially, if not materially, inferior goods and services.

The resolution of the issue of autonomy versus heteronomy, or network versus hierarchic organizations, depends on the assessment of resource use. The nature and availability of resources highlight the different views of the access and capacities that different kinds of organizations have with regard to their use. Many assume that most or all resources for housing are controlled by large organizations and that the essence of politics is therefore the struggle between 'public' and 'private' interests. A third 'sector', however, can be seen to control critically important resources over which the commercially or publicly 'corporate' sectors have little or no effective control. Namely, those resources which are of the person – imagination, skills, initiative, co-operation, and determination – and those material resources which individuals and households possess such as discretionary income, savings, or property in the form of existing buildings, land, materials, etc. The management and maintenance of dwellings and their surroundings, and therefore their longevity, depend primarily on the care of their residents and users. In most contexts the amortization of investments depends on the will of buyers and renters to undertake and implement contractual obligations. The most common motives for the investment of these personal and local resources are the satisfaction of simple material needs – which are neither commercial nor political even though all three motives are often mixed. Where use-values and motives predominate, the 'public' and 'private' sector labels are misleading and obscure the fact that so many resources are personally and locally controlled even where they are not personally or locally owned.

This *de facto* power of the 'popular sector' is obvious in the vast areas of non-commercial or only semi-commercial and officially unauthorized housing of most cities in rapidly urbanizing countries (figs 32, 33, 34, 35). Even among those who have similar assessments of the resources controlled by the three sectors, public, private and popular, there are still widely different assumptions with regard to capabilities for their effective use. Those with confidence in the superior capability of central organizations and the industrial technologies that only large organizations can support, will naturally suppose that the problem is how to incorporate the resources of the popular sector in centrally administered programmes (of housing action in this case). On the other hand, those who have less confidence in the hierarchic organizations and heavy technologies of the 'formal' sectors, and more in the network organizations and light technologies of the 'informal' or 'non-corporate' sector, will see the problem quite differently. For those who take the general positions of this book, the improvement of housing conditions and the ordering of urban development depend on the maintenance or re-introduction of local control through government guarantees of access to those resources which can only be used, or that are best used by people at local levels.

These opposing attitudes and perceptions of the relative capabilities of people and institutions of the formal and informal sectors are emotionally charged, but they are not necessarily based on subjective factors. Although difficult to measure, it is easy to observe how people behave and everyone has experience of the critical tendencies that can lead to the conclusion that effective control over housing, anyway in the longer run, should be in personal and local hands. In the first place, it is generally if not always true that the personal will to act depends on the expected consequences. Few if any willingly pay an exceptionally high rent for an exceptionally poor dwelling – one must be forced to do so by scarcity or police powers. As soon as these are relaxed, prices will decline. One's tolerance for

32

33

34

Figs. 32, 33, 34, 35. Squatter settlements on four continents illustrating the common scales of direct housing action by low-income urban people. At the time of writing, about one-third of the population of Caracas, Venezuela, were living in *ranchos* (above left; photo by Paul Coulaud); about half the population of Ankara, Turkey, were living in *gecekondu* (below left; photo by Mark Fortune); between one-third and one-half of the population of Lusaka, Zambia, were living in squatter compounds (above right; photo by Patrick Crooke); about one-third of the population of Manila, Philippines, were living in squatter settlements (below right; photo by Patrick Crooke).

35

undesirable consequences is more or less proportional to one's responsibility for the decisions that led to them. When these two facts of life are placed in the context of housing, or of any other complex system for the satisfaction of personally and locally variable needs, it is hard to see how the conventional positions on these issues can be maintained.

From the studies in Peru, Mexico and the United States, which are being followed up by further research, it is tentatively concluded that aggregated housing demands can be accurately estimated and projected, and that these can be effectively used for resource and infrastructure planning, but not for housing programmes. The clear implication is that the latter are inappropriate instruments of housing policy and, ideally, should be abandoned altogether. In practice, of course, this cannot be done until all sectors of the demand can be appropriately housed by locally controlled systems and this goal may never be reached in any large and complex society. But, an immediate start should be made to the reduction of public investments in direct housing construction and a concomitant increase of investment in infrastructure and basic resources.

The visible and frequent failures in centrally administered housing appear to be directly proportional to the levels of national per capita income and rates of population growth – although the increasing frequency of premature deterioration of public housing, so noticeable in Britain and the U.S.A., may modify this impression. In rapidly urbanizing countries with 'free market' and 'mixed' economies, it is rare to find that low income households are in fact housed in projects intended for them. When they are, it is common to find that the majority are in extreme arrears of payment for rent or purchase. Construction and management costs of publicly sponsored 'low-cost' housing schemes are often at least twice as much as the costs of equivalent housing built by the 'informal' sector (the financial cost differentials are far greater if debt servicing is taken into account as the latter uses little borrowed capital). Premature deterioration and vandalism, on the other hand, appear to be more common in wealthy than in poor countries, but this may well correlate with forms of tenure – publicly-sponsored housing in low-income countries is usually sold while most, if not all reported cases of deterioration and vandalism in Britain and the United States are of rental housing.[5] Prohibitions of illicit transfers and subletting, which are universal, are also far less effectively controlled in countries with low per capita incomes and budgets so that inappropriately assigned housing in these contexts is more frequently adjusted to meet real demands.

All such problems can be interpreted as consequences of the standardization of procedures and products which any large organization must impose in order to operate economically. The public institutions which have to satisfy political demands for appropriate uses of public funds are at an even greater disadvantage than law-abiding private organizations that have only to satisfy the demand for investors' returns. The latter may either build to specific demands of prospective occupiers or, and more commonly, build speculatively and sell or rent to the highest bidder. The public supplier is obliged to specify the demand as well, so that the chances of a successful matching are remote, especially when the decision-makers are culturally remote from the users of the goods and services they provide.

Neither the public nor the formal private commercial sectors can compete with an unfettered popular or informal sector housing system for the three reasons already given: first, because the network of independent operators provides the requisite variety of the 'controlling system' so

[5] Colin Ward, ed., *Vandalism*, Architectural Press, London, 1973

that locally and personally specific demands are more easily met; secondly, because the consequently greater expectations of satisfaction stimulate the use of available human and material resources; and thirdly, because personal responsibility and, therefore, tolerance are maximized. Not only do locally self-governing housing systems provide exceptional value for money and high levels of utility in proportion to resources invested, but when these resources are adequate, they generally create aesthetically satisfying and culturally meaningful environments. As pointed out at the beginning of this book, few designers or administrators of centrally administered housing prefer mass housing environments to those created by locally self-govering systems.

The issue of the desirability of local participation in housing depends on the answers to the following questions that are still open, notwithstanding the evidence and interpretations of this book:

1. What are the resources on which housing provision depends?
2. What sectors or kinds and levels of organization have access to and effective control over those resources?
3. What is the degree of requisite variety in housing for the various socio-economic and cultural sectors?
4. What sectors or kinds and levels of organization are capable of providing the matching degree of variety in the controlling system?
5. To what extent will participation increase tolerance for mismatches between users' priorities and housing actually obtained?

If the answers to these questions show that centrally administered systems have a greater potential than locally self-governing systems, then it follows that local citizens' participation is materially unnecessary and undesirable to the extent that it complicates administration and lowers productivity. These are certainly common conclusions and there is plenty of evidence to support the view that citizen participation in centrally administered housing programmes requires more time and money per unit of production when the whole process and all operations are accounted for. But if the answers show that locally self-governing systems have a higher potential for housing provision, then the issues and problems of the alternative forms of participation are relevant.

Alternative forms of participation

If citizen participation in housing is necessary it is essential that the participants and enterprises and institutions they employ should be free to use the resources available. Not only must resources such as building materials and equipment, manual and managerial skills, building land and financial credit be accessible, but their users must also be free to employ them in ways compatible with their own requirements without inhibiting the freedom of others. The same argument applies to infrastructure, for utilities and services providing access to sites – such as public transportation – and facilitating building and residence – such as mains water and electric power. As the division and distribution of levels of action and authority suggests, housing action by locally self-governing organizations rest on the basis of municipal services and both rest on the basis of regional or national authority over basic resources.

Authority and acton, or giving orders and carrying them out, are independently variable at all levels. And it is obvious as soon as these distinctions are made that the same combinations of decision-making and task-performance can have entirely different values and consequences at different levels of either organization and authority, or of operation and action. Different situations are generated by the possible combinations of the three levels of action and authority (Figs. 30, 31). The common and most questionable extremes highlight the critical importance of appropriate combinations: the modern tendency of central government, and even international agencies, to involve themselves in the detailed planning, building and management of people's dwellings, is complemented by another common and wasteful absurdity: the private determination of land prices by the aggregated decisions and actions. Both these peculiarly modern hybrids waste resources and increase scarcities by inflating prices or by providing unwanted or unusable goods.

The intermediate situations provide more positive examples. Utilities in towns are generally distributed through conduits that have both network or chequer board, and hierarchic or tree-form characteristics. The supply of mains water and electricity is from a central source, or a network of sources, and both have to be scaled down from quantities that could destroy individual users if they drew from them directly. In order for mains water or electricity consumers to have equal access to the supply, the major grids or networks must be centrally planned and administered. Metropolitan water boards or regional electricity corporations will not usually insist on providing installations in houses as this responsibility would create an uneconomic, if not unmanageable, bureaucracy. Intermediate organizations may take over before the supply reaches the individual consumer, or associations of consumers may co-operatively install or manage a local supply. This is relatively common and often highly desirable in localities with low incomes or difficult terrain. Many villages and urban settlements have successfully installed their own utility distribution systems – sometimes requiring excavation of trenches in rock, the modification of individual properties, or the careful co-ordination of works with local and domestic activities. Any of these can increase costs for an exogenous contractor to levels that put the product beyond local economic reach. For every successful case of community action of this kind, there are several unsuccessful ones, often involving people in considerable losses of human and material resources. Such failures are the most common way in which development potentials are inhibited and lost.

This last point highlights the importance of appropriate matching of levels of authority and action, as well as their dependence on local circumstances. While it is possible and helpful to generalize about the extremes, no simple generalizations should be made about the intermediate levels and the boundaries between all levels. Only in exceptional circumstances should central authorities provide local goods and services or should local residents control social resources. The practical problems of citizen participation, therefore, in housing or in any other complex activity, is to answer the above mentioned basic question in ways that fit particular circumstances: *Whose participation* in *whose decisions* and *whose actions?*

WHO DECIDES? \ WHO PROVIDES?	SPONSORS	USERS
SPONSORS	1. Sponsors decide and sponsors provide	2. Sponsors decide and users provide
USERS	4. Users decide and sponsors provide	3. Users decide and users provide

Fig. 36. Participation as a function of who decides what shall be done, and who provides the means. In conventional sponsored self-help housing projects (2) participants provide their labour; the most common form of self-help is neither sponsored nor authorized and the mass of the people decide and provide for themselves (3); in democratic systems, sponsors provide what users cannot manage themselves, within limits set by planning legislation (4).

By limiting the field to the sponsors of the activities and to the users of the goods and services produced – to government and lower-income people in most of the cases referred to – three significantly different contexts for participation are defined by the alternative combinations of decision-making and task performance by sponsors and by users. (Fig. 36). In the fourth, in which sponsors both decide and carry out the tasks, there is no participation in any of the usual senses. Each of the other three, however, can be illustrated at all levels of housing action.

Participation and Self-Help

Popular misconceptions of participation in housing tend to limit the field of discussion to the self-help construction of new dwellings. Recent and rapidly growing concern in Europe and the United States with the premature loss of existing dwellings is raising awareness of the fact that management and maintenance are equally or even more significant factors in housing than initial design, construction or even capital financing. The over-emphasis on new construction may be more reasonable in rapidly urbanizing countries. In many cities such as Bombay and Mexico, however, enormous losses of low-rental inner city housing through premature decay place heavy burdens on low-income sectors that need them most. It is an error to think that participation in housing is synonymous with self-help construction. This is reinforced by the false assumption that construction matters more than management and maintenance. New home owner-builders commonly save more money by being their own contractors even where labour is relatively cheap. Finally, the over-emphasis on dwellings diverts attention from the importance of participation in the provision of utilities and amenities and, although in less direct forms, from the importance of citizen participation in the planning and management of resources, as well as major infrastructure.

In the spreading and intensifying debate over the desirability of centrally administered housing schemes there is a danger that too little attention is given to the design of the subdivisions – the boundary and property patterns – and the relatively greater longterm consequences of alternative forms of management and maintenance. Frequently preferred forms of modern housing greatly reduce the potential for participatory management and maintenance, either by building forms that impede the physical separation of properties, that make co-operative work by non-specialists extremely difficult, and that make structural alterations impossible.

Sponsors Decide and Users Provide

Most sponsored self-help housing projects and programmes are of this type. While there are many variations, the most common is that in which the sponsor selects the site, plans the dwellings, and arranges the financing and administrative procedures before selecting the participants. Sponsors are usually governments in the many Latin American cases, but often private non-profit organizations in the North American and British cases. Participants in sponsored, aided and mutual self-help projects are sometimes self-selecting but more often this is done by the sponsor. It is unusual for groups formed by blood ties and chance friendships to be sufficiently homogeneous for the standardized financing, construction procedures and building types required. Variations are possible and often introduced, but they complicate the administration and therefore tend to slow the programmes down and raise costs. In one Latin American guide for self-help housing, 25 distinctly different administrative operations are recommended, many continuing throughout the project, such as keeping up the morale of the self-build teams and keeping accounts of hours worked in addition to the more complex scheduling of building operations that involve higher proportions of unskilled labour.

The same principle is maintained where managment or maintenance is carried out by users according to sponsors' procedures and instructions, but the only cases known to the writer are in the United States. One is a turnkey programme where tenants with prospects of becoming owner-occupiers were required to prove their qualifications by taking responsibility for maintenance.[6] The other is the case of tenant management in St. Louis, Missouri,[7] in which the tenant-managers, elected by the tenants, are employed by the housing authority. While the results of the former were equivocal, the latter programme, which is perhaps too recent for evaluation, appears to be very positive.

In all these cases, the participants are more or less passive contributors to the sponsor's enterprise although, as in the last case, it may have been initiated by the participants in the first place. Consequently they may maintain attitudes more commonly associated with self-governing systems. It is also evident in some evaluated and well administered self-help projects in the USA (Fig. 37) that the closely supervised and even paternalistic administration of the construction phase may be a

[6] These opinions are based on an unpublished 12 volume study for the US Department of Housing and Urban Development, Washington DC, 1970. The extensive field studies were directed by the author in collaboration with Ezra Ehrencrantz, of Building Systems Development, and under the supervision of Donald A. Schon of the Organization for Social and Technical Innovation. Many of the principal findings were summarized in *Freedom to Build*; most of the co-authors were members of the OSTI team. A volume in the series on self-help in management and maintenance was prepared by Carla Okigwe.

[7] Further relevant work on tenant management in the USA has been carried out by Robert Kolodny, Department of Urban Planning, Columbia University, New York City. The project described is the subject of a 16mm sound film by Marion Anderson, *The Walls Come Tumbling Down*, The Ford Foundation, 1975. The most recent and relevant work on tenant management in Britain, including a summary of Andrew Gilmour's study of experience in Norway, is Colin Ward's *Tenants Take Over*, Architectural Press, London, 1974

37

Fig. 37. Single-family houses built by Mexican-American ex-migrant farm workers in California. This is one of many aided and mutual self-help housing projects administered by Self-Help Enterprises, a private non-profit corporation funded by the US government.

necessary preparation for the future owner-occupiers' independent management and maintenance.[8] In contexts where sufficient skilled voluntary assistance is available, as in the United States, resources generated or mobilized by sponsored participatory programmes certainly have greatly exceeded any exceptional initial investments. The sponsoring organizations in the successful cases known have been small and private, although funded by public agencies. They have, therefore, been able to use highly localized and personal resources in ways that large self-help housing programmes cannot – unless local field personnel are so highly motivated that they will work exceptional

[8] A volume on aided and mutual self-help housing was included in the unpublished study of self-help housing in the USA (see footnote 6). This was prepared by Beatrice Levine and Hal Levin and focussed on an in-depth evaluation of the programme administered by Self Help Enterprises Inc., of Visalia, California.

hours and are encouraged to do so by their superiors. The generally small self-help projects in Britain and the USA are varied and, as they build or improve single-family homes in almost all cases, they are highly adaptable. Participants' tolerance is generally high in these projects, if only because they are rarely, if ever, conscripted so that the decision to build is their own, even if they have little control over the design or building procedures.

Where conventional self-help housing programmes have been administered directly by central agencies, and where they were in large projects, results appear to have been less satisfactory, if those that the writer has seen (mainly in Colombia) or been personally associated with (in Peru)[9] are representative. The scarcity of field personnel and the often excessive demands made on their time in the poorer countries inevitably heightens the political and economic necessity for rapid and large-scale results. Projects are therefore large in most cases, and highly standardized in form and procedure. In poor countries where unemployment is rife, participants who are usually at the higher end of the low income sector are less motivated to put in their own manual work since local labour is cheap. Opportunity costs for the participants, therefore, tend to be relatively *higher* than in wealthier countries. In many if not in most cases, high proportions of 'self-help' builders are paid substitutes. Deprived of the opportunity to make savings by self-mangement, these costs are merely transferred to the sponsors most of whom include them in the subsidy. Given the artificially lowered prices, and the extreme scarcity of housing of any adequate kind, there is rarely any lack of apparent demand for participation in sponsored, aided and mutual self-help housing programmes. Substantial areas of the Ciudad Kennedy project in Bogota were built by government aided self-help

[9] John F. C. Turner, *The Re-education of a Professional*, in *Freedom to Build*, op. cit. ch.7

to standard designs (Fig. 38). Five years later most of the houses had been partly demolished and rebuilt (Fig. 39). Wastage of this kind can largely be avoided, of course, if the obligatory and standardized work is limited to a 'core' unit which owner-occupiers can subsequently add onto as they wish. But there is no way in which centrally administered participatory programmes of this kind can make full or even reasonably adequate use of many of the resources commonly used by unaided self-help builders.

An example of spontaneous community action in an urban-industrial country is provided by the case of Black Road, Macclesfield, in the industrial North of England.[10]

Users Decide and Users Provide

One owner-occupier in an older urban neighbourhood scheduled for redevelopment not only shared many of his neighbours' strong feelings against the scheme, but he was also convinced that the houses could be rehabilitated at much lower cost than the planned redevelopment. Neither his own family nor his neighbours were opposed to the replacement of the old and obsolete houses, so much as to the dispersal of their local community. Knowing how similar schemes had affected friends and relatives in the recent past – especially older people – many feared rehousing more than the often unhealthy conditions of their present homes. Ideas about an alternative rehabilitation scheme therefore interested a large enough number of the neighbours to start working out the details of the alternative and to start convincing the others and to interest members of the local authority and the local press.

The usual diversity of residents in an older neighbourhood, and the mix of owner-occupiers, leaseholders, tenants and sub-tenants, compounded the

[10] Michael Hook, *Macclesfield: The Self Help General Improvement Area,* in the Architects' Journal, 12 November, 1975

38

39

Fig. 38. A street of lower- and moderate-income houses first built through aided and mutual self-help, administered by a government agency, in Ciudad Kennedy on the outskirts of Bogota, Colombia. This photograph was taken shortly after completion.

Fig. 39. A similar and neighbouring street in Ciudad Kennedy, five years later. Most of the houses built in the aided self-help programme were subsequently rebuilt to higher standards by the individual households on their own unaided initiative.

difficulties of improving very obsolete terrace houses of varying condition and degrees of deterioration. Many occupiers were older people, a few very old indeed. Some, especially the eldest, were entirely dependent on their old-age pensions, while several of the youngest were also quite poor, though with expectations of higher incomes. In spite of all these problems, all the participants' houses were modernized and major improvements were also made to the jointly owned, semi-public access paths, garden, and parking space.

The development could not have taken place without the sympathetic reporting of the local press and the active support of the local health and planning authorities; nor, of course, without the unified demand of the residents themselves. The community leaders' skills in ensuring these supports were the first pre-requisite and these could not have been exercized without the respect and confidence of those with whom they had to deal. With these resources, and the predisposition of a sufficient number of individuals from the different sectors and institutions concerned, it still took over a year to obtain the necessary support to launch the proposal formally.

Naturally, there was considerable opposition to be overcome, especially the explicit challenge to the local and central authorities' development plans and, even, to their policies. Well documented evidence on the comparative economic as well as social benefits won the day – backed, of course, by the confidence generated by the proposers' own competence and determination. They were also assisted by the current swing of public opinion against redevelopment projects, already reflected in the attitudes of the participants themselves, and by the tightening economic situation and increasing likelihood that expensive redevelopment programmes would, in any case, be drastically cut back.

Having obtained agreement in principle on the scheme

with the authorities concerned, the first practical step was to arrange for transfer of all the properties to their occupiers – and most of them were tenants. Without the leverage of threatened compulsory purchase at very low prices as the only alternative, it would have been impossible to persuade the landlords to sell at prices their tenants could afford, even with assistance. Both purchase prices and improvement costs, however, were covered through the imaginative use of different forms and sources of financing – enabling even the old-age pensioners to participate in the scheme.

The works to be carried out varied from house to house because the houses and terraces were different and in different conditions and because the demands of the highly varied households were different. No general building contractor would take on such a complicated and risky job – with owner-occupiers in residence during the work – for an economic price. The only way to keep costs down was for participants to act as their own general contractor and to deal with each job and operation separately so that adjustments could be made as the work proceeded and all the unforseeable problems arose. These many problems and, above all, the concurrent inflation of building prices forced the participants to do more and more for themselves in order to keep costs down to the level of their finances. As the group was its own co-operative general contractor, each participant was free to do what he or she was able to on the job, and those who were unable, like the very old, could be helped by the others. Some carried out major alterations and additions, others did only the minimum necessary to bring their houses up to the minimum standard. Every one of the several dozen houses differed in some important way and yet all were successfully completed within a reasonable time and at costs all could afford – well below the cost of new houses, and far below what the work would have cost if carried out in any other way.

Not the least achievement is the enormously increased sense of personal and community pride and capability. Vandalism and premature deterioration while these people remain in residence are inconceivable. And the probability of their dealing with other problems that might overwhelm their neighbours is proportionately greater.

Users Decide and Sponsors Provide

The principle of user decision and sponsor provision has been well-established by private developers and higher-income owner-builders or new home buyers whose properties are publicly serviced. In cities where these conditions are common, this principle is being extended to those who most need these services and who are most deserving of the subsidies (not to mention the capital gains) that they commonly represent. Large-scale utility installations have been made in legalized squatter settlements in Peru since 1962 and similar programmes have been carried out elsewhere. In their earlier forms, however, centrally administered improvement programmes are only indirect responses to popular demands. Where these are interpreted by central policy-makers, planners and administrators, and where the projects are not carried out in direct response to locally specific demands, as many problems can be created as solved, particularly in the short run. Great care must be taken, therefore, to distinguish between generalized programmes responding to general demands, and specific projects carried out by central agencies in response to particular local demands.

In the Peruvian programmes and the similar large-scale project in Mexico City described in the third and fourth chapters, standardized specifications and procedures can create considerable and unnecessary hardships for the intended beneficiaries and even lead to the failure and loss of the capital investments made. Cases where publicly adminstered projects have brushed aside offers of complementary assistance by local residents and have then been suspended before completion for lack of funds, are all too common. Worse still are the cases, as in that of the mason's family discussed earlier, where residents of the mandatory improvements are saddled with debts they cannot afford to amortize or which they are unwilling to accept, either because they have other priorities or because they do not believe they are getting adequate value for their money. The only way in which major mismatches of the mandatory supply of improvements and the priorities and effective demands of the residents can be, and often are, resolved is by the exodus of the poorer residents who sell their appreciated capital to higher-income households able and willing to afford the improvements made. But of course those displaced will merely recreate the 'problem' which the sponsors set out to solve in the first place.

Such problems can be avoided, as some more recent Peruvian experiences have shown. In one major new settlement, with a site assigned by the central government, well over 100,000 inhabitants were served with graded streets, electric light and power and water mains serving public standpipes in the initial stages of settlement and in consultation with the settlers' association which formed an effective provisional local government.[11] The costs of such simple and basic installations can generally be borne either by the inhabitants or by the government – or by a combination of public subsidies and local contributions. Where local associations are made responsible for ensuring residents' payments or even collecting them themselves, agreements are far more likely to be honoured.

The above illustration describes the principle of public response to local demands in terms of infrastructure. The same principle applies, of course, to other components of the built environment and to supporting institutions. For

[11] Nicholas d'A Houghton, in The Guardian, London, 23 May, 1972

many years in Peru and in other countries, some public services have been provided as a matter of course in any established settlement, irrespective of its legal status. It is a tradition in Peru, for example, for local communities, whether rural villages or urban settlements of the kind described, to build their own schools and for the Ministry of Education to staff them. Waiting communities may often run their own schools with voluntary or even salaried teachers. In recent community development programmes, the same principle has been applied to tools and materials as well as technical assistance, especially in rural areas.

Central Planning and Local Control

While there are many possible answers to the central question – whose participation in whose decisions and actions – the cases quoted reflect and support my own conclusion that the most effective and necessary forms of participation are (1) central authorities' participation in local housing development through actions that ensure personal and local access to essential resources (including the freedom to use what is locally and personally possessed) and (2) citizen's participation in the planning of resources and infrastructure (on which local housing development depends) by central authorities.

The problem of how these are achieved in practice, and how they could be introduced where they are not practised, has been only partially examined here and I do not presume to have more than a few clues to the answer. One of the most important (which has been partially developed in chapter Six) is the distinction between the two basic types of control: those that set out specifications of what shall be done and lay down procedural *lines* to be followed, and those that set *limits* to what may be done leaving the actor free to find his own way within those limits. The difference is illustrated by the contrast between the community action programme at one extreme, and the conventional centrally administered project at the other – the credit borrower can do what he and his household wish as long as they build a house within given material limits, eg, above certain minimum requirements for design and construction and within a certain period. The successful applicant for a project unit, on the other hand, is tied to a given location, a standard unit with a standard form of tenure and mode of payment. While the former can combine his loan with any or most of his own particular resources to achieve the best match that he can manage with his own household priorities, the latter must adapt to what is given and use other resources for other ends or lose the opportunities they represent.

In addition to the critical matching of appropriate levels of authority and action, and the selection of the consequently appropriate form of participation, it is also essential that the right control system is adopted. Prescriptive planning and administration are essential for the design and installation of major utility systems, for example. The necessary hierarchy of a piped water supply system can provide limiting parameters for the development of the dwelling environments they support. But the application of the same principles to the dwelling environments within the areas defined will inhibit local and personal initiative and therefore deprive society of a major part of the resources available for development.

9. A PROGRAMME

This conclusion to *Housing by People* is an introduction to the further action I now consider essential. The plan for thought and research and for action and development outlined in this final chapter is written as an invitation to correspond with me and to meet for discussion whenever opportunities arise.

Housing by People – like my previous book *Freedom to Build* – is addressed primarily to those who share and believe in certain principles and methods. The dozen or so other writers with whom I have co-authored publications during the past ten years are a small minority of the members of this world-wide and rapidly growing school of thought and action. It can be identified by a common recognition of policies with a small p, and of the issues and positions, principles, and practical methods that have been outlined in this book and which are presented for discussion.

The plan for further thought and action is addressed to those who take the radical positions on the issues summarized and who are therefore also inclined to think and act in accordance with the principles and methods that follow.

Value, Economy, Authority

On the issue of *value* – in housing or in any other activity generating personal goods and services – the choice is between the values of what procedures and products *do* for people and their environment, and the material values of the things themselves. In other words, it is the issue of *use-value* versus *market-value*. Many tend to take exclusive positions on this point – denying one or the other. Most will agree that use-values must always take precedence when conflicts arise, but will accept the necessity for market values as the only known means of ensuring personal and local choice in a complex society. (However, this does not imply an endorsement of laissez-faire or unconstrained market economies).

Those who recognize the fact that use-values lie in the relationships between people and things – and not in things themselves – will recognize the significance of alternative means by which alternative ends are sought. This is the issue of *economy*. If primary values and ends are functional and defined by performance (that is, use rather than quantities), then economy must have as much to do with the means of production, as with productivity. Economy of means implies resourcefulness, or getting the most from the least. And in a densely populated planet it must also mean maximizing the use of renewable and plentiful resources and minimizing the use of non-renewable or energy-intensive, heat-generating resources. Those who confuse economy with material productivity make a dangerous error. Like market-values, industrial production has its uses but these must be limited or industrialization will destroy mankind even more surely than the primitive capitalism that generated it.

Those who see this point are bound to recognize the issue of *authority* which determines the choice of means and which are used to achieve the ends. When economy is understood as resourcefulness, technology is obviously political as it is a matter of who controls resources and their uses. The central issue raised in this book is that of *who decides?* Who decides, and who provides what for whom is clearly the political issue of power and authority.

The conclusion presented in the preceding chapter was that local control over existentially relevant activities (such as housing) and central planning (of locally scarce resources and supra-local infrastructure) are complementary. But centralized control of resources will only lead to totalitarianism. As the contemporary experience of urban settlement in the poor countries so overwhelmingly shows, people and their local institutions and enterprises control *de facto,* though not in law, by far the greatest proportion of resources for housing. And as repeatedly pointed out, central agencies possess and have direct control over mainly non-renewable and polluting resources. There is, therefore, a *de facto* balance between local and central powers and spheres of activity. When a critical mass of people realize this, the structural changes vital to the immediate improvement of the condition of the poor, and to the continued existence of human life, can take place. The breakdown of traditionally accepted institutions in urban-industrial contexts testifies to the fact that this development is equally likely in rich societies.

Three Principles for Practice

The three principles discussed in chapter Six are the necessary basis for any viable housing policy. First, there is the necessity of self-government in local affairs for which the principle of local and personal freedom to build must be maintained. Second is the necessity for using the least necessary power, weight, and size of tools for the job (whether managerial or technological). In principle, this is to say small is beautiful, but with the proviso that some jobs – especially the less beautiful ones – do need large organizations and powerful machines. Thirdly, there is the principle that planning is an essentially legislative, limit-setting function, and must cease to be confused with design, which has to do with laying down lines of action. No generally known and recent thesis deals with this necessary principle of proscriptive law in housing and environmental planning, but readers receptive to the principle will immediately recognize it in the syndrome of the categorical programme.

The great majority, if not all, housing, building and planning agencies, and most of their professional and administrative agents, are locked into the procedural and conceptual assumption that government housing actions are categorical programmes. That is, a specific category of goods and services for a specific category of users. Any new or newly perceived problem, therefore, is promptly seen as a demand for a new programme. So, as one North American analyst observed, public housing policies consist of an ever-increasing aggregate of closed actions, each creating new problems and demands for even further programmes. Those who adhere to the principle of limits must reject housing projects and programmes as viable ways of solving housing problems. But, of course, while we may agree that house building agencies must change their roles or be abolished, this cannot be done overnight without causing major disruptions in which the poorest may be the greatest immediate losers.

Four Proposals

With the above assumptions a clear programme emerges for thought, research, action and development. Before making further observations on these discrete elements, and as my main purpose is to initiate activities, it is best to start with the proposals themselves.

The first and most important proposal is to increase communication between people in action. All over the world there are many people practising these principles – in fact there are millions who are exercizing their freedom to build and there are vast arcas of housing by people. Among them are many who see far beyond the obvious facts and immediate potential – especially those who have come up against the often disastrous public and private corporate action for ordinary people. They have therefore come to question the principles on which heteronomous (top-down or centrally administered) housing is based. And a rapidly increasing number are preparing or already carrying out radical alternatives. No single activity can be more important than encouraging these pioneers. Increased inter-communication will not only help the redoubling of their current efforts but will greatly increase the chances of gaining support from currently inactive people who want to work in these ways. Material and administrative support is already coming from an increasing number of public and private, national and international agencies who are seeking to restructure their policies.

Proposal One is to *set up an international communications network in order to intensify the use of existing channels of communication (both formal and informal) in ways that increase universal access and reduce the risks of exploitation by centralizing powers.*

By far the greatest need and the most frustrated demand is for case studies and materials. Data banks tend to be counter-productive, partly because they are undiscriminating and fail to distinguish data from information so that the user is overwhelmed with facts that obscure as much as illuminate. Furthermore, data banks are technologically opaque to all but the experts, most of whom are employed by agencies that flout all the principles the network supports.

Proposal Two, therefore, is to *set up a number of centres where case materials will be collected, indexed and made available to those needing access to the precedents set. All such centres will be interconnected so that anyone can search the rest for particular documents or topics.*

There is an inherent conflict between data and information – but selected and informative data depends on the values adopted and the concept of the relevant universe.

There can be no information without theory. If the principles and methods presented here are indeed basic, then there is an implicit theory. The job of those who share those principles and methods, therefore, is to elucidate that theory. This is the 'school' referred to in the second paragraph of this chapter. Many of those who are conscious or unconscious members of this school, especially those who do not have day-to-day responsibilities for practical action, are struggling with new concepts – with the attempt to build models that will truly reflect the realities they see. I am among those whose efforts are spent mainly in this task.

Proposal Three is to *institute a new school of the built environment: not to create a new organization, but to establish the fact that there is such a school and that it exists by virtue of many scattered individuals and a few groups and small organizations. The medium of the school is the international communications network.*

The fourth, but by no means the least important, is law. Those who accept the principles in general will also agree that significant housing action by central agencies is necessarily in the legislative sphere. If it is true that categorical programmes and projects evade the real problems, and therefore tend to exacerbate the problems they are intended to solve, and that their material effectiveness is directly proportional to the increase of centralized power, then the rewriting of law must be a major concern. The production machinery is at fault and attempts to accelerate it are counter-productive. This is where attention must be focused. Current housing and planning law is largely prescriptive – and as emphasized above, the greater part of housing action consists of closed or categorical projects and programmes and these are actually referred to as laws! Such monstrous absurdities must cease, but before they can be eliminated the concept of liberating and decentralizing proscriptive law – the concept of boundaries and limits – must be re-instituted.

The Fourth proposal, then, is to *initiate a programme for the design of proscriptive law that will generate self-governing form.*

The current state of the science and art of building construction has permitted the formulation of performance standards which, instead of imposing specifications, sets limits of required performance, leaving the specification to the imagination and skills of the designer and builder. But the state of current social, economic and environmental sciences is relatively backward or, perhaps more accurately, disorganized. It is therefore difficult to know the laws governing the use and management of space, and the social and institutional as well as the truly economic nature of its provisions. As laws cannot be written for processes or systems that are poorly understood, this vital task depends on the development of more accurate and complete theoretical models of the built environment.

Four Methods

The tasks to be carried out emphasize their interdependence. In order to further clarify these relationships to identify the critical methods linking the four main tasks, and in order to clarify the issue of the specialists' roles, the model of the proposed research and development plan is elaborated below. (Fig. 40) The basic figure is the Geddes square used earlier (Fig. 21) to relate practices, problems, issues, and principles.

Each pair of adjacent tasks or activities belongs to a different 'sphere' with significantly different properties from the others. Information and theory belong to the scientific/academic sphere in contrast to action and law which are of the political sphere (executive or administrative and legislative). It is common experience

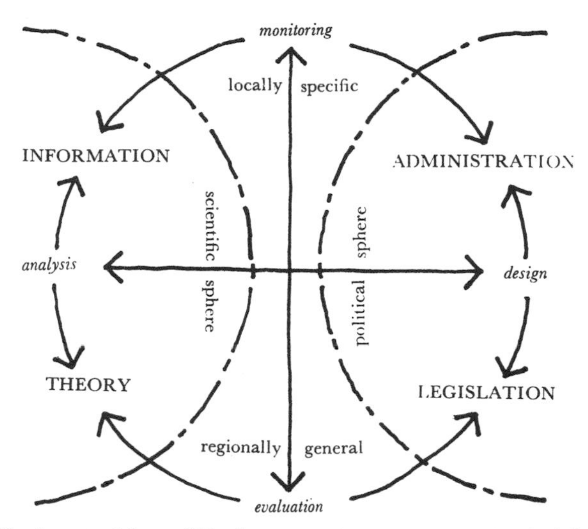

Fig. 40. *The elements of change.* Whether explicit or implicit, consciously recognized or not, action generates and is generated by the experience of previous action and administration, information, theory, and norms – which may be habits or customs or laws and regulations.

and knowledge that administrators cannot abide theorists in their midst. Administrators of any kind, whether football team captains or housing managers, will appreciate the motto which an editor of a once famous political newspaper posted behind his desk: *'don't confuse me with the facts, my mind is made up'.* He was referring more to interpretations than to news itself. Like all administrators he required detailed information feed-back, but only insofar as it permited him to regulate the progress of the job being administered. Few, if any, administrators have the power to change the ends of work in progress. So any interpretation of the feed-back that questions their goals is of no use to them. Only the strategic staff can use such information, because as they determine actions occurring over longer periods, they have time to change the rules and the ends.

Similarly, detailed information is of little direct use for strategic planners or those charged with the information of law – the legislator needs explanations of how things work.

Only empirical prescriptions or specifications can be written from raw data on past experience (which in fact constitutes the bulk of planning and housing law). Principles, limits, proscriptive law or performance standards require theory or generalized models.

In order to understand their complementarity, the scientific and political spheres must have recognized 'connectors'. Monitors record action in the field and supply administrators with relevant information – such as financial accounts. Similarly, evaluators interpret models to the lawmakers. Monitoring and evaluation are often confused. They are quite different although complementary methods. Monitoring is a continuous activity providing information on progress or change enabling administrators to adjust their operations so that they do not exceed the financial or other limits set. Evaluation, on the other hand, is a periodic activity providing assessments enabling strategic planners or legislators to adjust policies and reset limits for future operations.

Although it is often attempted, as in the now fashionable but complex attempts at cost/benefit analysis of environmental impacts, evaluations cannot be made from data that has not been selected and organized conceptually. In other words, evaluations confuse measurable indicators with use-values – which seems to be difficult to avoid in conventional cost/benefit analysis – their evaluations will be no more than descriptions at best. These are likely to be excessively detailed and uninformative, however, and therefore likely to obscure the use-values that people actually hold.

The essential differences between action, information, theory and law must also be recognized. Actions and information are specific to time and place. Theory and law must be general to be useful. While there are obviously considerable variations there must always be this relative difference between the two spheres in any particular context. The failure of categorical housing projects and programmes is due mainly to the tensions created by imposing generalized specifications on different people and places; conversely, the failures of contemporary housing and planning law are due to its excessive specificity.

The differences between all these elements have been blurred so that none of them serve their real purposes. Norms and laws have become hopelessly confused with operations and programmes; the inevitable result is the fusion of legislative and executive powers and the creation of the heteronomous state. Issues and theory have become confused with problems and information. The inevitable result is intellectual chaos and isolation – we oscillate madly between the absurd extremes of excessive generalization and insistence on the uniqueness of our own experience and the irrelevance of history.

The vital connecting links between the local and general spheres of activity are analysis and design. The analyst tests theory against information while the designer translates norms into specific actions. And, of course, analysts and designers are complementary and mutually dependent as monitors and evaluators. As the monitor depends on the evaluator (and theorist) for guidance in the selection of data to collect, the analyst depends on the designer to indicate the models to be tested.

The programme suggested here is for immediate action by those who share these disturbing views and who are therefore anxious to come to terms with the situation by action on it.

ABOUT THE AUTHOR

John F. Charlewood Turner was born in 1927 in London. He followed his father's footsteps to St. Edmund's School, Surrey, Wellington College, Berkshire, and the Architectural Association School of Architecture, London, enrolled at the AA in 1944 and after interruptions including a year in Italy with Belgioioso, Peressutti and Rogers, obtained the AA Diploma in 1954. He lived in Peru from 1957 until 1965, working mainly for Peruvian government housing agencies in the promotion and design of community action and self-help housing programs in villages and urban squatter settlements. He lived in Cambridge, Massachusetts, from 1965 until 1973 during which time he was associated with MIT, first as a research associate of the Joint Center for Urban Studies of MIT and Harvard University and subsequently as a lecturer in the Department of Urban Studies and Planning. During this period he wrote many published articles on housing and urban settlement in Peru and other low-income countries, lectured extensively, and acted as consultant for national and international agencies, mainly in Latin America.

In 1970-71 John Turner directed an evaluation of self-help housing in the USA under Donald Schon for the U.S. Department of Housing and Urban Development. Some of the main findings and conclusions of this were published by members of the team in *Freedom to Build* which he edited with Robert Fichter (Macmillan, New York, 1972). Since moving to London in 1973 with his second wife and two younger step-children, John Turner has been working at the AA School and the Development Planning Unit of the School of Environmental Studies, University College of London.

His most recent consulting work has been in India, East Africa and the Middle East. He is an active member of the Centre for Alternatives in Urban Development at Lower Shaw in the borough of Thamesdown, Wiltshire, where his colleague Peter Stead is promoting people's freedom to build and manage their own housing. He now looks forward to corresponding with others concerned with the issues of freedom to build and of housing by people.